POWER
MÖVES

POWER MÖVES

LIVIN' THE AMERICAN DREAM, USA STYLE

KARL WELZEIN

itbooks
AN IMPRINT OF HARPERCOLLINSPUBLISHERS

*it***books**

Kayfabe, smarks. This book is a work of fiction. References to real people, events, establishments, organizations, or locales are intended only to provide a sense of authenticity, and are used fictitiously. All other characters, and all incidents and dialogue, are drawn from the author's imagination and are not to be construed as real. I mean, there's no way anyone could have really done any of this crap, right? Kinda concerning.

HarperCollins books may be purchased for educational, business, or sales promotional use. For information please e-mail the Special Markets Department at SPsales@harpercollins.com.

FIRST EDITION

Designed by Ruth Lee-Mui

Library of Congress Cataloging-in-Publication Data is available upon request.

ISBN 978-0-06-223323-3

13 14 15 16 17 DIX/RRD 10 9 8 7 6 5 4 3 2 1

*Dedicated to the good people of
Michigan and the '84 Detroit Tigers.
Bless You Boys.*

CONTENTS

ATTN: BOOK 4 SALE. $$$. POWER MOVES.
DECEMBER 1, 2012   ix
A Note from the Publisher   xiii

1   Can't Wait for the Weekend!!! APRIL 15-MAY 7, 2010   1
2   The Big Situation MAY 9-17, 2010   6
3   Karl vs. The Carlsons MAY 18-JUNE 20, 2010   13
4   Dave JULY 5-OCTOBER 3, 2010   23
5   2 Live Karl DECEMBER 2, 2010-FEBRUARY 4, 2011   30
6   Back in the Saddle with Ann FEBRUARY 5-27, 2011   62
7   Hold On Loosely, But Don't Let Go
     FEBRUARY 28-APRIL 22, 2011   78
8   Gotta Take Advantage APRIL 26-JUNE 11, 2011   105
9   Dad's Day and Crazy Cooter JUNE 13-JULY 14, 2011   123
10   The Heat Is On JULY 15-27, 2011   136
11   Captain Karl's Pizza Ship JULY 28-AUGUST 4, 2011   145
12   Vernon AUGUST 10-22, 2011   154
13   Brenda and Condolences to David
     AUGUST 25-SEPTEMBER 26, 2011   161
14   Enter Jody, Exit Activia SEPTEMBER 27-30, 2011   180
15   Jody and Big J OCTOBER 1-19, 2011   186
16   Karen and the Big B-Day Celebraish OCTOBER 20-24, 2011   199
17   McRibboween OCTOBER 25-NOVEMBER 4, 2011   205
18   Holidays and the Head Honcho
     NOVEMBER 11-DECEMBER 26, 2011   214

     Acknowledgments   241

ATTN: BOOK 4 SALE. $$$. POWER MOVES.

DECEMBER 1, 2012

'Sup, book company. Name's Karl Welzein, hailin' from Grand Blanc, Michigan. Sometimes it feels like people forgot about Michigan. Me, I like it just fine, thank you very much. 'Round these parts in Grand Blanc and Flint, there's pretty much always a rockin' celebraish goin' on. And we've got everything you could want in a big-city lifestyle, but with down-home comfort. Chili's, 'Bee's, golf courses, tons of bars. The works, really. Full spread. Michigan built this country on rock 'n' roll, badass cars, and great spots for a vacay with plenty of lakes and babes galore. Plus, Bob Seger was born here and still calls it his home. And if Michigan is good enough for Bob Seger, then it's damn sure good enough for me and should be good enough for ANYONE else. Plus, when they finally get Detroit back up and runnin', man, people'll be lined up to move to the mitten. That's why I got my spot all picked out and warmed up. I'm a Michigan man, and I bleed Tiger orange and blue.

A couple years ago, I was gettin' real steamed from puttin' up with all kinds of family crap, and really bein' held back from my true calling as the President and CEO of Bad Boy City, USA. Always figured I'd make a good writer 'cause I got all kindsa ideas about business, entertainment, and rockin'. Plus, I had some guy feelins I needed to sort out. So I started puttin' pen to paper, sometimes wrote stuff on my Dell (My roommate Dave broke like two of 'em. Idiot. Had to get the files transferred. Real hassle), Arby's bags, on TP in the john, a few walls in our pad, the fridge, some spots on the

Internet, just tellin' my story. Then, a little while ago, I gathered it all up as much as I could and thought, man, it's like I've been gettin' cooler than ever, and maybe it's time for the world and the USA and everyone to see how stuff isn't so bad sometimes if you just keep rockin' with the heat of a thousand suns.

Sadly, there's a bunch of stuff in here that talks about crap you wouldn't expect from such a cool customer like myself. Mostly in the BM department. But that's a part of life, I guess, and if you wanna tell a true story, you gotta include the nasty parts. Let's face it, usin' the john is a major time for reflection on the world around us. Am I right? Anyway, you have to "push" through those parts to get to the light at the end of the tunnel. Ha! (Just some guy humor there.) Maybe you could edit some of it out or make me look more sensitive? Babes dig a sensitive man, you guys. To be honest, I'm keepin' it chillin' with primo babes from coast to coast, and pretty sure they'd still be down to rock, especially when the book comes out. Authors are some of the boldest bad boys of all time, and everyone knows babes crave their carnal touch for the mind AND bod. (I'm doin' pretty righteous in the bod department, you guys. No complaints from ANY babe.)

So, back to the USA. Man, since we're pretty much #1 in the world for everything, I think it's important to see how a REAL bad boy handles things around here. The country might be better than ever right now, with opportunities, new eats, and booze drinks with bold flavors like never before, and the babes are so out of bounds you just gotta dip your shades to have a peep. Think Kid Rock said it best with "Chillin' the Most." That's exactly what the USA is doin'.

Sorry, think I might be kinda bombed. Feel like I could drink a thousand beers right now. Gotta focus. Kinda lost track of what I was talkin' about. Guess my point is, is America lookin' for the next bad boy author? Well, he's right here, amigos. And you're holdin' the pages in your hands. So let's make this a go and get $$$ like never before, you guys.

United We Rock,
Karl Welzein

P.S. If you could get Bob Seger, Kid Rock, Guy Fieri, Stone Cold Steve Austin, Kirk Gibson, or Ric Flair to write the foreword, that'd be off the chain.

P.P.S. Just leave all the dates and crap in. Otherwise it won't make sense to people readin' when things are happenin' and how time goes forward. Don't understand why all books aren't like that. So stupid. Save a lotta writin' for no reason.

A Note from the Publisher

Dear Reader,

The book you now hold in your hand is, perhaps, one of the most terrifying glimpses into the lows of American culture ever presented. Offered in an unflinching and entirely unedited manner, *Power Moves* is the life and times of a man who, for all intents and purposes, represents what our country has become.

We felt compelled to publish this ethnographic study of Karl Welzein, this everyman, in his natural habitat of Michigan in order to show just how far our country has fallen in the realm of consumerism, gluttony, and reckless abandonment of good health.

We present this book as a cautionary tale. It is not meant to laud the boorish and inappropriate behavior of this man. Instead, we hope that with this publication we have created a document that will impress upon every American that we can and should be clinging to the ideals of our forefathers with all the strength we can muster, before our country is destroyed.

We do, however, find this book highly entertaining.

Kindest regards,

The Publisher

1

CAN'T WAIT FOR THE WEEKEND!!!

APRIL 15-MAY 7, 2010

THURSDAY, APRIL 15, 2010

Really lookin' forward to the weekend, you guys.

Was thinkin' about getting the boat out if it isn't too cold. You never know what the weather's gonna be. My wife Ann keeps sayin' that we should think about sellin' the boat because we didn't use it enough last year. You can't use a boat when you spend every weekend at Target or some dumb friggin' birthday party. It's such BS. Didn't say that to her, but it's true.

I was out tinkerin' in the shed last night and found an old Pam Anderson *Playboy*. Been waitin' for Ann to hit Target again so I can give it a good flip-through. Feels like I never get any alone time to do what I want. Dang, forgot what a babe Pam was. Really smokin'.

SUNDAY, APRIL 18, 2010

This morning I was supposed to go golfin', but Ann's mom was late for brunch so I missed my tee time. I hate that cow. Was really lookin' forward to givin' my new Callaway driver a whirl. Ann saw the charge for it on the Visa statement and got all in a huff. She said we need to discuss big purchases. She must spend 400 dollars a week at Target and I've never heard a word before the plastic gets swiped. Why is it ok for her to buy a cart full of crap that adds up to a wad of cash, but if I treat myself to one nice thing that costs a pretty penny, I catch hell for it? Sick of this. I could sure go for a few cold ones at Chili's. Really steamed and need to cool off.

At least I still have racquetball tomorrow.

MONDAY, APRIL 19, 2010

Stuff that sucked today:

1. Had to cancel racquetball. Forgot one of my two daughters has a dance recital. Goin' to a dance recital instead of racquetball makes me wish I had my guy tubes tied.
2. I'm sick of that Mexican guy at Subway judging me when I ask for ranch dressing on my footlong meatball sandwich. This is AMERICA, Tito.
3. Looks like they firewalled the *Maxim* website at work. I'm a grown adult, I can look at whatever I want to on my break. There's no nudity in *Maxim*, and it's good to have a nice laugh in the middle of the day.
4. Just found out everyone at work calls me "The Clogger" behind my back. Feelin' kinda down. It only happened once.

TUESDAY, APRIL 20, 2010

Stopped at 7-Eleven for a Breakfast Big Bite this morning. All Ann ever makes for breakfast is Cheerios. Cheerios don't stay with me all morning. There's no protein. It's not brain food, and I work hard. When I was gettin' back in the car, someone opened their door into the Sebring and dinged it. I just had it washed too. It made me so P.O.'d, I spilled mustard on my shirt. Should've just went home and called it a day.

WEDNESDAY, APRIL 21, 2010

After work tonight, I was supposed to meet up with the guys at Hooters in Bay City. It's a monthly tradition. But Ann left the windows down in the Cherokee and it rained, which means two hours with the wet/dry vac and no Hooters. Really sucks. I know she does things like that on purpose. Sick of this.

While I was cleanin' up the mess, Ann "surprised" me with a "cheer me up." Skechers Shape-ups. Such a cheap shot. Why doesn't she just call me a fat loser to my face? What if I gave her some Lane Bryant underpants? I'd never hear the end of it.

Skechers Shape-ups look like slow-kid shoes. I'd be a dead man if my bro Al saw 'em.

After I finished up with the Cherokee, I was fishin' around in the freezer and found an old box of Costco mozzarella sticks. Was super pumped, but Ann made me throw 'em out because she said they were too old. So stupid. THEY'RE FROZEN!

WEDNESDAY, APRIL 28, 2010

Was really lookin' forward to the weekend. I was supposed to shoot 18 on Saturday, but Ann said we had to shop for new jeans for me. She said I need "nice" jeans for a party at the Carlsons. "Nice" jeans sounds like "dork" jeans to me. I'm just fine with my Wranglers. They're such a classic and really comfortable. Ann doesn't know what cool is. I needed to mellow out, so when she went to Pilates, I went in the shed and toked down a roach from my golf bag that was left over from my bro Al's bachelor party. I got WAY too high. Figured that the weed wasn't even good anymore so I hit it pretty hard. Then I ate a whole pack of deli ham that was supposed to be for "lunches only." My son saw me actin' weird and asked, "What's wrong, Daddy?" I felt so ashamed for gettin' stoned that I went and cried in the downstairs guest bathroom. Guess my emotions are just kinda runnin' high lately.

When Ann got home, she saw how I ate all the deli ham and knew somethin' was up. Kicked me out of bed for the night.

Yeah, like me sleepin' on the family room sofa is punishment.

We have Cinemax.

THURSDAY, APRIL 29, 2010

It looks like Ann is gonna parlay my little weed escapade into a Sandals vacay. Can't wait to see her bod in that ruffled old-lady one-piece! Plus, that means I have to use up the vacation days I was saving for my Vegas trip with the guys. I really screwed up huge.

FRIDAY, APRIL 30, 2010

Woke up this morning and saw that the damn dog took a huge crap on the carpet. Had to clean it up and missed my tee time before work. Then I pulled my groin lifting the wet/dry vac. Weekend: ruined. Wouldn't have happened if the kids would take him out like they're supposed to.

People ask me sometimes why I don't talk about my kids more. I have a son (Mama's boy, cries all the time) and two daughters (who hate me).

That's why.

I'm going to water the backyard and drink a cold one. So sick of everyone.

SATURDAY, MAY 1, 2010

We had to go to Ann's sister's for her disgusting homemade pizza tonight. It was EXACTLY how I wanted to spend my Saturday night. Havin' to eat that garbage with a smile makes me want a gun in my mouth instead. I work hard all week so we can have nice things like Papa John's. Just because her sister and that freeloader Terry are broke doesn't mean I should have to suffer.

FRIDAY, MAY 7, 2010

Gettin' so sick of bein' pushed around. I wanted to watch *Die Hard 2* on the new Blu-ray player tonight, but Ann just said, "I don't think so," and put in a Diane Keaton movie like I didn't even have a choice at all. It feels like every day I lose a little bit of "me." Ann used to be down for action flicks anytime and we'd have cocktails every night. But after the kids came along, it's like I disappeared, unless they needed a punching bag to gang up on. Sucks feelin' alone, you guys.

2

THE BIG SITUATION

MAY 9-17, 2010

SUNDAY, MAY 9, 2010

It was supposed to be Ann's big birthday celebration tonight. I had everything planned out: steaks, plenty of thoughtful gifts, potato salad, sheet cake. The works. Full spread. There must have been a delay at Amazon though because none of the gifts showed up. Then I burned the steaks 'cause my son was showing me some stupid card trick and if I leave in the middle of it he starts with the water-works.

Ann spent most of the night in the bathroom, fake crying really loud. GODDAMNIT, I TRIED MY BEST, GIMME A BREAK! After a few hours, she left and said she was going somewhere that she's appreciated. I didn't know Kohl's was open so late.

MONDAY, MAY 10, 2010

Tonight, I had to meet Ann at Panda Express to "talk things over" in private. Nothing gives me diarrhea more than "talking things over" except for maybe Panda Express. The whole thing was a disaster. I spilled orange chicken on my favorite Chaps polo, and it looks like we worked things out.

TUESDAY, MAY 11, 2010

They bought us a free Quiznos lunch at work today. I really overdid it. Took down two whole Chicken Carbonara subs. Now everyone's calling me "Carbo." It's embarrassing, but it's better than "The Clogger," I guess. And it's not like I ORDERED two. There was an extra. What was I supposed to do, let it go to waste?! Sue me because I care about the environment.

All that Quiznos really came back to haunt me. But you know what I always say, "Ain't much in this world a little cologne can't fix."

WEDNESDAY, MAY 12, 2010

On the way to work today, a button popped off in the middle of my shirt and my stomach hair kept sticking out. There's this cute new gal at work that I'd been waitin' to make a good impression on. She caught me playing with my stomach hair and said, "Gross."

I decided to make a run to Kohl's at lunch for a new shirt. I take pride in my appearance. Picked up this bad boy:

PRETTY MUCH THE MOST BAD ASS TEE I'VE EVER SEEN.

It was pretty much the most badass tee I've ever seen. Kohl's really stepped up their game. They only had a large, so I needed to squeeze into it. It was kinda hard to breathe, but everyone's into the slim fits now. Sometimes pain and discomfort is the price of fashion. Plus, it made my arms look awesome! Pretty sure the cute new girl noticed. I went and did some pushups in the john to max out my bod and get real beefy. When I got home from work, Ann said, "What's with the new T-shirt, Slim? Hot date tonight?" Then she started laughing her ass off like she was watching that Raymond jerk's television show. My daughters kept calling me "The Situation" or something and crackin' up in their room. I don't know what that means, but I got real sick of it. It went on for about an hour. Then Ann started calling me "The Big Situation" and all of them had to go out on the deck they were laughing so hard.

I was sick of their bullcrap and went to Chili's bar to cool off with some cold ones. I don't need their abuse.

THURSDAY, MAY 13, 2010

Woke up in the garage this morning. Guess I overdid it. Chili's has these top-shelf margs that just go down so smooth. There should be a warning on the menu: "Caution: Top-Shelf Margs go down REALLY smooth."

I don't remember last night at all. Apparently I knocked the flat screen off the wall and now we only get channel 7. Ann said I put on some Allman Brothers really loud in the family room and then tried to microwave a whole box of Jimmy Dean breakfast sandwiches. AND I bought cigarettes. Smoked half a pack in the house. I haven't smoked in six years. Looks like I'm in pretty hot water with Ann and the kids.

I was supposed to head down to Comerica for the Tigers game with my bro Al this weekend, but Ann said that she "already informed" me that we have the family picnic for my son's soccer team on Sunday and that I never told her about the baseball game. It's such crap. She frickin' KNEW. I don't know why I'd have to go the stupid picnic anyway. I never go to the stupid boring games. Plus, I already bought these bad boys to wear to the Tigs:

Ann doesn't need to know how much they cost ($279!!!). She doesn't know what Maui Jims are anyway. Ann has zero taste.

Ann says she would've let me go to the Tigers game if I wouldn't have "made a real clown" out of myself last night. Yeah right. She's such a liar. Maybe I wouldn't act like such a clown if Ann didn't let the kids call me stuff like "Captain Pig-Out" at the dinner table! Two helpings of spaghetti is NOT "overdoing it." I'm eating in the family room from now on. And also, "let" me? I'm a grown adult. I should be able to do what I want, Ann.

I was really bummed about the Tigers game. Couldn't sleep. Stayed up late watching channel 7. Ordered *The Best of Soul Train* DVD collection. So smooth, you guys.

SATURDAY, MAY 15, 2010

They let us out of work early yesterday. Friday rocks! Everyone went down to Paddy McGee's at the Jewel for $2, 24 oz. drafts. Was supposed to take it easy—I had movie plans with Ann later. I started havin' a blast though. When cold 2x4s are just 2 bucks, it's important to take advantage of the savings. Gotta watch out for your bottom line in this economy.

I kinda lost track of time. Cold ones were going down so smooth. Missed the movie by about two hours. Just completely forgot. When I got back to the house, Ann was locked in the bedroom, and I was too hammered to care. I screamed through the door that she should've just went without me. Doesn't make sense why I have to sit next to her for HER to enjoy a movie. PLUS, I was at a WORK outing! How does she think we pay for nice things like going to the movies? With her eBay business? It's total crap.

Ann made me so upset that I couldn't properly digest the Reuben I had at Paddy's. Paddy's does a really good Reuben. Piled high with corned beef, kraut, Swiss, and their special sauce. Served with your choice of potato. Always hits the spot.

Ann always knows just how to ruin my night. I should've just stayed at Paddy's. I was havin' a NICE conversation with the cute new girl. That's something Ann wouldn't know how to do in a million years.

After I got back from Paddy's, I was fishin' around in my "secret stash" I keep in the basement. Found an old copy of the *SI* swimsuit issue with Kathy Ireland on the cover. Reminds me of the cute new girl if she really hit the gym:

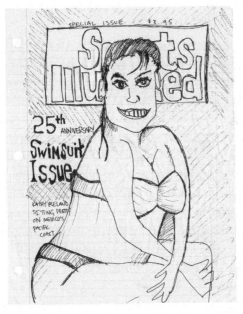

MMMM-HMMM!!! Sure don't make 'em like Kath anymore, you guys.

Ann finally came out of the bedroom and immediately went into how I couldn't go to the Tigers game. And if I DID go, not to bother coming back. Fine with me, I WISH I could live at Comerica Park. Me and Al have big plans for a pregame at Cheli's Chili Bar across the street. Cheli's Chili is pretty much the best in the world.

Yesterday was a doozy. Me and Al didn't get to the game until the 3rd inning. We got a little lost on the way. Too many roadie Gin-and-Tonics (I like to call 'em G&Ts), I guess. Then, 15 minutes after we sat down, some scumbag Red Sox fan kicked Al in the back and spilled nachos and beer all over his shorts. We were gonna whoop his butt but decided he wasn't even worth it.

Ann said my son cried at the soccer picnic because I was the only dad not there. And that's EXACTLY why I didn't go.

I kept asking Ann if she was mad at me for going to the Tigers game yesterday, and all she kept saying was "No, it's fine" with that fake smile she makes. You know the one, where women make that crazy Joker smile with their mouth and then they have mean eyebrows. Makes her look like a psycho. Ann's SO irritating. If she only knew all the looks I got from babes in my Maui Jim sunglasses yesterday. AND she's ticked off that I spent almost $400 at the game. Like I fine-tooth comb every trip she makes to Target.

PLUS, I spent some of that money on T-shirts and caps for her and the kids. It isn't my fault that I forgot 'em under my seat. Guess the thought doesn't REALLY count.

So sick of this.

3

KARL VS. THE CARLSONS

MAY 18–JUNE 20, 2010

TUESDAY, MAY 18, 2010

Ann was still steamed last night and went to bed early. Finally got to see *The Hangover*. She wouldn't ever let me watch it, said it's "barnyard humor." Ann doesn't know anything about today's comedy. It rocked! Man, if I wasn't stupid married, I'd party like those guys every night.

Today's the cute new gal at work's b-day. I wore my new rockin' tee. It shrunk a little bit in the dryer, but if I don't stand up straight, it's fine. Gotta look good. We're all supposed to go out to do somethin' special after work.

Ann says we're supposed to go to ANOTHER dance recital for one of my kids tonight. I'm puttin' my foot down. Not going. They make me feel creepy. I don't understand why Ann says it's "gross" when I look at half-naked women in *Maxim*, but it's totally fine when they're underage at a dance recital.

Was gonna fake "I have diarrhea" to get out of it. It gets you out of anything. Work? Church? It's always foolproof. Think I'm gonna save it though. Goin' with "stuck at work," which is code for "stuck at the bar at Chili's for the cute new gal's b-day."

Came home from work tonight and crashed out on the couch. Ann called me a "lazy sow." It was Hump Day!

I had a few glasses of wine at lunch. Just the little bottle Sutter Home 4-pack from the party store. Kept it light. It's European, helps you relax, and lets you digest your food properly. Plus, I paired it with a new Artisan Bread sandwich from Quiznos. It's inspired by Europe. So good. Ate it in my car. Europeans love to dine outside. Got a little snoozy from the lunch wine, so I kicked it into gear with a few sips of Wild Turkey out of my "secret flask." That's how the Europeans do it to stay sharp after their vino. Guess I overdid it though 'cause I woke up in my car a few hours later. Went back in to work and everyone was gone for the day.

Ever think how diarrhea is just butt barf? Jeez Louise, I'm still sauced.

Really lookin' forward to the weekend, you guys.

Was in the john tryin' to multitask and change the battery in my Seiko. Dropped it in the toilet. I was already "done with my business," so it was a disaster, couldn't really just grab it out. Had to flush it. Ann gave that Seiko to me for our anniversary last year. I'm gonna be in hot water when she notices it's missing. I gotta play it cool. Thought I'd do a little pre-damage control and made reservations for us at Applebee's for tomorrow night. Called Ann to tell her. She said, "Wowwee, Prince Charming. Who said romance is dead?!" Then Ann started laughin' so hard she had to hang up the phone. I was just tryin' to do somethin' nice. Felt kinda down so I decided to go for a drive after work. Just wanted to be alone for a while.

When I got home, everyone was glued to some *Grey's Anatomy* crap and didn't even notice I was late. No one said anything until a commercial break long enough for Ann to inform me that the family voted, and I was only allowed to use the basement john from now on.

So sick of this crap.

FRIDAY, MAY 21, 2010

Applebee's sucked my ass tonight. Sorry to swear, but it sucked my ass.

Had to leave work early with "diarrhea" so I could hit Paddy's for a few pregame cold ones just to get through it.

Me and Ann were SUPPOSED to go to Applebee's alone. But Ann invited the Carlsons. Can't stand Doug and Tina. Ann made friends with Tina at some Curves class she went to (once) and now they have to be OUR friends. Well, they're not MINE. And I made those reservations so we could do somethin' nice together, not listen to Doug talk about his back problems. Plus, Doug's always tellin' Ann how "great" she looks. Creeps me out. AND they both kiss hello on the lips. For my appetizer, I ordered the Spinach & Artichoke Dip and only got about half of it. Ann made me share MY appetizer with the table. Doug and Tina are so cheap. They shoulda got their own. Then, right in front of the Carlsons, Ann told me I should get one of the "Under 550 Calories" meals 'cause I "overdid it" on the dip. Spinach and artichoke are VEGETABLES! Ann doesn't know anything about home-cooked food that you don't just heat up. I had to save face so I got the Southwest Jalapeno Burger. Added on chili cheese fries. I should be able to get whatever I want. Ann just had a stupid salad. So weak.

For dessert, I ordered a double Blue Coconut Marg. Ann shot me a look, like she's better than me, THEN ordered a Triple Chocolate

Meltdown and shared it with Tina. They wouldn't shut up about it. Of course when the bill came, the Carlsons didn't chip in for it, or the appetizer, or the tip. Just paid for their entrees. And Doug didn't get ANY drinks. He's such a load.

Got into a pretty nasty screamin' match with Ann on the way home about my "behavior." No idea what she's talkin' about. Ann acted like it's MY fault that Doug and Tina suck.

I'm goin' on the deck for a cig. Sick of this crap!

SATURDAY, MAY 22, 2010

If Ann plays that Kid Rock/Sheryl Crow "Picture" song ONE more time, I'm gonna kill myself. Every time we get in a fight, I swear she does it to torture me. If you're gonna play Kid Rock, at least play somethin' that ROCKS. Jeez.

And Ann invited the Carlsons over for steaks tonight. Wonder what kind of belt is best to hang myself with? Guess who has to leave the house to BUY the steaks? Here's a hint: It's not Ann or the Carlsons. I was all settled on the couch watchin' muscle car auctions. I had plans. Now MY Saturday is shot.

SUNDAY, MAY 23, 2010

Don't think we'll be havin' dinner with the Carlsons again anytime soon. Guess I got blackout drunk on margs and gave Doug a piece of my mind. He said he likes his steaks "well done," not "well don't." They were MEDIUM RARE and grilled to perfection. Then Ann started laughing hysterically. I told him, "Well, DON'T come over anymore then, you fat mooch! Stay home with your wife tied up in the yard where she belongs!"

Tina started crying and ran out. Doug went after her. Good riddance. I guess Tina's been on medication that makes her gain weight and she's "really sensitive right now." What is she taking? Oreos? Ann said they won't even answer her phone calls to apologize. Now she's "so embarrassed" she can't even look at me. Perfect! Maybe I can enjoy my Sunday now. I earned it after that Friday and Saturday bullcrap.

MONDAY, MAY 24, 2010

Ann still isn't speaking to me. Gonna kick back and eat some cold cuts in peace.

TUESDAY, MAY 25, 2010

Ann found out I ate all the cold cuts so she hid my laptop adapter as "punishment." She makes no sense! Besides, I paid for those cold cuts. They're essentially MINE that I'm generous enough to GIVE to the kids.

Ann wanted the checkbook so she could go to the store for more. I told her, "I don't know where it is. Looks like it's gonna be a PB&J week." To prove my point, last night I ate all the variety pack "lunches only" chips AND all the granola bars.

When I got home tonight, Ann told me she "accidentally" washed my Maui Jims in the laundry! They're all bent and scratched. Really steamed about it. How did they "accidentally" get in the washer?! They were in my sock drawer in their case when I left for work. When I called her out on the "accident," she said, "Oh, must be like how you accidentally ate all the kids' lunch chips and granola bars." I PAID FOR THOSE AND I CAN EAT ANYTHING I WANT, ANYTIME I WANT TO!!!

I don't care if we just had supper two hours ago. I'm going to Wendy's for a Jr. Bacon and a Frosty.

WEDNESDAY, MAY 26, 2010

Ann's all excited about *Sex and the City 2*. Don't get why. I told her, "If you're so into it, why don't you try to get hotter like the blond slutty one?" Shouldn't have said it in front of the kids. Now we have to schedule a "talk" for tomorrow morning. I asked her why we couldn't just have it right now. She said, "I can't even look at you. I'm going to bed." Great.

Samantha wouldn't do that. We'd go to bed and she'd take care of business. Downtown. Like adults. Plus, the *Sex and the City* gang would really get on Ann's case about those clogs she lives in.

THURSDAY, MAY 27, 2010

Tonight was make-your-own-taco night at the Welzeins'. Really overdid it. I just couldn't stop. They were goin' down so smooth. Took out three soft shells and five hard shells. Plus chips and guac. Can hardly move. Ann said I was "beached" on the couch. I said, "You're a beach." Didn't fly very well. Then she got on my case about helping with the dishes. She's so lazy. Loading the dishwasher is not a two-man job. That's why I bought it!

WEDNESDAY, JUNE 2, 2010

Cut my hand pretty bad on Sunday tryin' to clean the grill. Needed stitches. I got some pain meds and Ann's been nursing me on the couch. I am MILKING this. Had homemade chili for supper in front of the TV and got to watch WHATEVER I want. Ann says I can't drink on my medication. C'mon. I'm only gonna have three at the most. She's runnin' to the store for milk in a minute. Brewski time!

THURSDAY, JUNE 3, 2010

Stayed up too late watchin' Tigers highlights on ESPN. Really draggin' today. Had a big weekend planned, but looks like I'm gonna have to cancel my tee time due to the hand injury.

FRIDAY, JUNE 4, 2010

Dunna dunna dunna, they say it's your Friday! Dunna dunna dunna, Happy Friday to ya!

Ann's going to her sister's to watch movies tonight. I'm supposed to watch the kids. No problem. I'll be hammered. Ann says I shouldn't drink while I watch the kids. She also says I shouldn't take a whizz behind the garage. Ann says a lot of dumb crap.

Gonna get some of those Vortex Miller Lites. They make it look like you're drinkin' a tornado. Super pumped.

SUNDAY, JUNE 6, 2010

Friday night I polished off a 20-pack of those Vortex Miller Lites and crashed. Ann came home and found the kids eatin' all the Pizza Rolls. Ann said it'd be best if I got a hotel room Saturday night. I told her I went to the Comfort Inn, but I really stayed with my bro Al. His wife was outta town. Had such a blast! We ripped through two more of those 20-packs and grilled up some NY strips. Yeah, real punishment, Ann.

When I came back this mornin', Ann asked if I learned my lesson. I put on my best puppy-dog eyes and said, "Yes." Could tell she felt really bad. Ann thought I was gonna cry, but I was just hungover. She's such a sucker. The only lesson I learned is that Vortex Miller Lites go down SO smooth.

Why do I only have a great weekend when I'm kicked out of the house? Really makes you think. Time for some soul-searching.

Monday. Great. Ann's makin' us a salad and baked skinless chicken breast for dinner. Great. My son needs help with some over-the-summer school project. Great. We're out of beer. Great. Ann said we're starting "no TV Mondays." Great. I never bought that gun to shoot myself. Great. We're supposed to go for a "family walk" after we eat. Great. Just GREAT! GREAT! GREAT!

Hump Day fever! Bruh nuh nuuhhh! Hump Day fever! Bruh, nuh, nuh, nuuuuhhhhh!!!

Headin' to BW3's for "Wing Wednesday." I just made that up!

Wing Wednesday was a disaster. I ate way too much and had to go home sick. Took today off. Just gettin' up and around. Tryin' to sip Pedialyte. Every time Ann looks at me, she just shakes her head. I'm SICK! It's not my fault it's coming out both ends.

Just heard Ann say to the kids, "That's why he's only allowed to use the spare bathroom." Now they're laughing. Really hurts, ya know?

I tried to explain how I took down almost three DOZEN wings. Ann said, "Am I supposed to be impressed?! Wow, real macho man! Just go sit on your potty." She doesn't get it. I'm sure there's lots of women who'd be into that. I'm gonna go lie down. Feelin' kinda spinny again.

On Friday, I was still a little dehydrated and I didn't feel so hot so I took the day off again. Ann went to Target and I got bored so I drank a sixer. When she came home, I was hunched over the tub with my pants down. Ann walked in and said, "Oh, you piece of shit!" Then just left. Didn't come home 'til late. When I asked her where she went, she said, "I was at SHUT UP, Karl!" Then Ann locked herself in the bedroom.

On Saturday, Ann got up early and left again. She left a note that just said, "Watch the kids." I dropped them off at *Iron Man 2* and went to Paddy's to relax. Got kinda caught up talkin' with Carly the bartender about how things are at home, so I was a LITTLE late pickin' them up. They called Ann's cell phone for a ride. She freaked out and called me. I said I was at Paddy's and was comin' to get them right away, which was true! She said, "Don't bother, Karl. Have fun."

Now Ann's doing this fake nice voice and makin' that crazy fake smile face. I feel lonely and sad. I try my best. My weekend is ruined.

Never thought I'd wish I was at work.

MONDAY, JUNE 14, 2010

My back's really hurtin' today from sleepin' on the couch. Kinda hoped Ann would cool off and stop bein' such a big bag o' bitch, but when I got home, there was a note that said her and the kids were "at Applebee's," like I should be jealous. I can go there whenever I want because I'm an adult.

Oh, poor me. Guess I'll have to drink some beers on the deck and grill myself a few brats. Boo-hoo. Oh, what will I ever do without my WONDERFUL family to get on my case? I hope they just decide to live at Applebee's forever.

TUESDAY, JUNE 15, 2010

Passed out on the deck last night. Woke up when the sprinklers came on at 5 a.m. Can't believe Ann just left me out there. Feel like crap today.

They need to change "for better or for worse" to "for worsefor worstest." Sick of this.

SUNDAY, JUNE 20, 2010

Things aren't goin' too well at home. I'm just tryin' to lay low. The Carlsons were over for dinner on Friday. Ann was tryin' to smooth things over. I got pretty bombed on margs and I guess I made a move on Tina in the kitchen. I don't remember it. Ann knows. I'm screwed.

4

DAVE

JULY 5-OCTOBER 3, 2010

MONDAY, JULY 5, 2010

Me and Ann were havin' some problems, I guess, so I moved out. Been crashin' at my buddy Dave's place. Had a blast on the 4th. Felt good to be free.

I've known Dave since high school from seein' him around at parties. We were never really friends 'cause he wasn't part of the cool crew, but I ran into him at Paddy's a couple months ago and he said he was "cleanin' up on the singles scene." If I ever wanted to hang, just "give him a ring." Guess he's an assistant manager at the gas station, so he meets a lot of new babes all the time. Pretty cool? Everyone else I know is bogged down with kids and wives and crap, so it seemed like a good time to connect.

TUESDAY, JULY 6, 2010

Dave's place ain't so bad. It's a little messy, but I sprang for cable and Internet. Ann's been really cold and hasn't called me or anything.

WEDNESDAY, AUGUST 4, 2010

Dave spilled Faygo on my laptop. Just got a new Dell. Back in business.

I put on a few lbs. livin' with Dave. Lots of frozen pizzas. They always hit the spot. Ann always said they were for "weekends only." Not anymore. We don't have "rules" at the new pad. Might buy a chin-up bar though, so I think some of the weight might turn into muscle. Gotta stay in shape.

THURSDAY, AUGUST 5, 2010

Did ten push-ups this mornin'. Feelin' jacked! Good timing, Ann wants to meet with her attorney. Think it's a bluff. Either way, wait 'til she sees how good I look! Can't wait. Got some new jeans today too:

Ann's gonna flip!

Also, picked up a bottle of Tim McGraw cologne. Ann LOVES that guy. Wait 'til she gets a whiff, she'll be BEGGIN' to have me back. Just tried some on, and man, I smell SO good.

Just noticed that Dave ate all my T.G.I. Friday's frozen potato skins. Looks like my night's ruined. Thanks a lot, "roomie." Really burns me.

FRIDAY, AUGUST 6, 2010

Gettin' pretty sick and tired of Dave rankin' up the john every morning before I have to get in the shower. Same thing, every day. He walks by and says, "Time to make the donuts." It was pretty funny a few times, but now it's gettin' stale.

Just got some good news though. Ann called to say that the kids have plans and don't wanna see me this weekend. YES! TGIF! Me and Dave are gonna go to Paddy's at 5 for drinks and some laughs. Time to par-tay down! Hope that cute Heather is workin'. Picked up this new tee at lunch to wear tonight.

Can't wait to see if Heather likes it!

SATURDAY, AUGUST 7, 2010

Holy crap. Me and Dave got WASTED last night. We got Wendy's on the way home but forgot to eat it. It's still in the car. Probably still good, right?

Went to check on the Wendy's. Might be questionable, but looks ok. Shame to see it go to waste 'cause it's Wendy's. Might just scrape off the mayo, then put on some fresh Hellmann's. When I was out there, I noticed that the front left panel of Dave's Skylark is dented BAD. No idea how that happened.

SUNDAY, AUGUST 8, 2010

Dave just ate a whole Little Caesars $5 Hot-N-Ready right in front of me and didn't offer me even one slice. He's a real greedy gross-out sometimes. And now he's watchin' that *Jersey Beach* show. The babes are kinda hot, but it's so stupid. Dave's always hoggin' the tube. I pay for the cable! Gonna go eat some of that Wendy's. Stashed it in the veggie drawer so Dave wouldn't see it.

MONDAY, AUGUST 9, 2010

Thank God Monday is over. It's Whopper night! Gonna go double Western, double mayo. I need the protein for my workout. Might go for twelve push-ups tonight. Feelin' pretty good about my bod.

TUESDAY, AUGUST 10, 2010

Think I cracked a tooth on a Corn Nut this morning. Guess my teeth aren't strong enough to handle BBQ Corn Nuts in the a.m. I called Ann for the dentist's number and told her what happened. She couldn't stop laughing and said she'd call back later. Pretty rude. Now I have to eat this whole Quiznos sub on the other side of my mouth. Hope Ann's happy.

I mighta overdid it on the Orajel. Just dribbled beer all over my shirt. Dave called me a "slob." Big talk from a man who has an old Hooters T-shirt for a pillowcase.

THURSDAY, AUGUST 12, 2010

Guess Dave smoked a bunch of grass, got the munchies, then ate three pot brownies before I got home. Idiot. If we have to go to the hospital tonight, I'll be P.O.'d!!!

SUNDAY, AUGUST 15, 2010

Me and Dave just arm-wrestled to see who has to clean the bathroom. I really crushed Dave just like Sly Stallone in *Over the Top*. Wish I still had the VHS. Such a great flick. Ann sold it at a garage sale for 50 cents 'cause I never watched it. Well, I wanna watch it now. She has ZERO taste when it comes to the classics. You don't just SELL *Over the Top*, you guys.

THURSDAY, AUGUST 19, 2010

Ann asked if I could watch the kids for a few hours on Sunday. Too bad, I'm busy. Looks like she won't be havin' lunch with her sow friends at Olive Garden. I'm doin' them a favor.

FRIDAY, AUGUST 20, 2010

Super pumped for the weekend! Goin' perch fishin' with Dave. Gonna bring a BIG-ASS cooler of Busch Light AND some egg salad sandwiches. CAN'T WAIT, CAN'T WAIT, CAN'T WAIT!!!

Split my pants at work today. Stapled 'em back together. Turned out ok but then the staples got snagged on my chair. Stood up and ripped out the whole seat. Full moon. Had to wait for everyone to leave. Went and found some old wood glue in the supply closet. It was a disaster. I got wood glue everywhere and it wouldn't dry. Kinda looked like I messed myself. Sick of this. I'm supposed to meet Dave at Paddy's and he's already there. Gonna go to Kohl's to pick up these bad boys. Hope the new bartender at Paddy's likes 'em. Friday on!!!

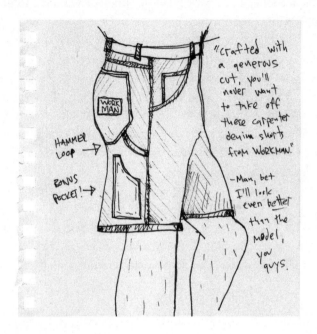

TUESDAY, AUGUST 24, 2010

Yesterday was a real doozy of a Monday. Got in a big screaming match with Ann on the phone. No one at work knew we were havin' problems. Guess they do now, and frankly, it's none of their beeswax!

WEDNESDAY, AUGUST 25, 2010

Dave just called me at work to ask how to unclog the toilet. Yeah, like I know. Gave him Ann's number.

FRIDAY, SEPTEMBER 3, 2010

Friggin' Dave downloaded a bunch of porn on my laptop and it froze up. Had to take it to Best Buy with "Black on Asian Anal Teens" stuck on the browser. Now I know he uses my computer to slap it around when I'm gone. So gross. Don't know how much longer I can stand livin' with Dave.

SUNDAY, OCTOBER 3, 2010

Been out of the loop for a while. I had a heart attack about a month ago when I was drivin' and crashed into a parked car. Been stayin' with Ann and the kids. Just tryin' to lay low.

5

2 LIVE KARL

DECEMBER 2, 2010–FEBRUARY 4, 2011

THURSDAY, DECEMBER 2, 2010

Me and Ann decided that since I was healed up from the "heart attack" (it was mild, didn't even really count) that I should probably move back in with Dave. Things weren't workin' out well for me at home anyway. Everybody was real nice for a while, keepin' quiet when I was watchin' football, treatin' me with respect and not makin' rude comments about my fitness or style, all the things I deserve. Then, about a month ago, Ann and the kids went to the mall, so I decided to kick back with a couple brews from my secret stash in the shed. "No alcohol" was part of Ann's "rules" while I was "getting well" and "living in the house." Other bullcrap included "no chips" and "us going to bed at the same time, 10:30." It was fine for a while when I wasn't 100%, but when I'm healthy, my body craves a few cold ones, some snacks, and a little nightlife. Not diet root beer, baby carrots, and early bedtime with my wife wearin' a flannel nightgown and covered in face crap.

So a few weeks ago, I had a few brews I stashed in the shed, started feelin' like my old self, and cranked up Van Halen's "Top of the World." I was doin' spin kicks, goin' bonkers, really lettin' loose.

Felt so good. I worked up a mean sweat and no one was supposed to be home for another hour, so I went down to just my unders and no shirt. It's nice to feel free in your own home. Just like a man.

Guess I lost track of time 'cause Ann and the kids came back earlier than I expected. I was on the floor doin' some badass Eddie Van Halen moves to "Poundcake" where you thrust your pelvis in the air and have your shoulders on the ground, wailin' on your axe. It's classic Eddie. The fly on my BVDs was a little stretched out though, and my peener snuck out. That's when they walked in and made a big scene.

Ann made me show her where my beer stash was and I had to dump 'em all out. My daughters started callin' me "perv" 90% of the time. My son started pullin' out his business in front of company, sayin', "I'm Daddy!" And there was another rule instigated, added to the list that Ann put on the fridge: "Trips to the store include the WHOLE family AND Karl."

Basically, they decided they didn't want me there anymore, and I agreed. Just need a little breather 'til they can appreciate me again.

FRIDAY, DECEMBER 3, 2010

Ate a whole XL Reuben Pizza at Paddy's tonight. The cute bartender thought I couldn't do it. She was really impressed and said it was "rad."

I was pretty hammered so I left to be responsible, but when I got home, Dave was in the john destroying it. I had to crap real bad, so I drove back to Paddy's. The BM pressure pretty much sobered me up. The cute bartender saw me come back in and said, "What, you miss me?" Didn't wanna just crap and leave, so I had five more Labatts to be polite.

TUESDAY, DECEMBER 7, 2010

Just went to get a late-night snack. Noticed Dave ate all my Bagel Bites. Stupid fat sow. Sick of this. Dumped all his cereal down the toilet to make it even.

WEDNESDAY, DECEMBER 8, 2010

Still mad that Dave ate all my Bagel Bites. They were a guarantee that I'd get to spend my first two hours of work in the john, away from everyone.

I just remembered it's almost Christmas. Don't know if I should get Ann a present. Really stressin'. Also, I don't know what to get the cute bartender at Paddy's. We've been kinda "buddy buddy" lately, I guess you could say. Just don't wanna give the wrong signals. Gotta keep it professional. I think I'll just hit a few places at lunch and see what catches my eye. I'm pretty much a natural when it comes to spottin' great gifts.

THURSDAY, DECEMBER 9, 2010

Got Ann one of those diamond heart pendants from that jewelry place at the mall. I asked her about exchanging gifts and she said I was welcome to buy the kids things, but it'd be weird for us to do that.

Boy, is she gonna be surprised about the pendant. I'm super pumped. Might even get to "stuff her stocking"? Ha!

FRIDAY, DECEMBER 10, 2010

10:37 P.M.
Just got home from Chili's. Really drunk. Miss Ann so much.

10:46 P.M.
Calling Ann. See what's goin' on. Calling Ann now.

10:49 P.M.
Ann won't pick up. Calling Ann back.

10:50 P.M.
Keeps goin' straight to voicemail. Callin' Ann again.

10:54 P.M.
Pick up, Ann! Stupid damn voicemail. Calling Ann back.

11:03 P.M.
Called back. Voicemail again. Calling back. Sick of this.

11:37 P.M.
Threw up. Sent Ann some sex texts. No reply. Dave said he does it all the time to gals. Never seen Dave with a woman EVER. Idiot.

12:06 A.M.
Called Ann. Voicemail again. Really steamed.

SATURDAY, DECEMBER 11, 2010

Guess I did somethin' really stupid last night before bed: drank a bottle of red wine and ate three bran muffins. This morning was just a nightmare. Every time I'd go in the restroom, Dave'd make gas sounds with his mouth. He's so immature. My stomach was upset! It's NOT funny.

The decent news is, Ann left a message that "we need to talk." Sounded like I called a few times last night, which musta been the right move 'cause she wanted to meet for coffee. My stomach was still upset though, so I spent most of the time makin' restroom trips. She finally just left without saying good-bye when I was in the john for the eighth time. Pretty rude. Coffee was HER idea.

When I got home, we were out of TP so I went to Paddy's. It's Dave's turn to buy it. Just 'cause I needed some right then doesn't mean it's my responsibility to supply it. That'd just encourage him bein' a cheapskate.

I was finally feelin' relief in the BM department so I took down the sampler platter and the Paddy McGee Sirloin. Plus, it was $12 buckets of domestics. Had to get two to take advantage of the savings.

Called Ann a few times to let her know I'm feelin' better. Thought she might be worried, but no answer. Straight to voicemail every time. Sick of this.

MONDAY, DECEMBER 13, 2010

Woke up late for work and saw the roof of the Sebring collapsed in from all the snow we got overnight. Had to drive to work with the top down in the 12-degree cold. Think my ears got frostbite. Don't know if I should go to the hospital.

When I walked into work all frozen, I heard a co-worker call me "Fatso the Snowman." Really hurt my feelings. Then Dave called me to ask how my car was. He said he piled the roof with snow as a "prank" like on that *Jerkass* show. Kept laughin' like an idiot. That's why the roof collapsed, NOT natural causes. Wanted to choke him through the phone.

Had to drive home with no roof. Might have been even colder than in the morning. And havin' the heat on didn't really do crap. I tried to take a hot shower but still couldn't get warm. Really P.O.'d at Dave.

I called Ann to ask her for advice about warmin' my body up and told her about the car. She laughed so hard she dropped the phone. Sick of this.

TUESDAY, DECEMBER 14, 2010

Had to go to the dealership to get the car fixed this morning. It took forever. So great. Way better than bein' at work. Plus, they had free donuts and TV. Some stupid old bag asked me to turn it down so she could read her book. Ignored her.

After the old bag left, they put on a fresh pot of coffee and I went in for donut numero ocho to celebrate. That place rocked so hard. I coulda lived there forever.

TV was stuck on one channel so I had to watch Dr. Phil. Man, what a dumb sack of horsecrap. "Yew shud do this! Yew shud do that!" He should do everyone a favor and shut his fat face. No one wants advice from some country pig man with a mustache.

When I got home, I had to make a mean coffee whizz and Dave was hoggin' up the john so I had to pee in the kitchen sink. Dave came out and freaked. Told him, maybe if he did the dishes like an adult once in a while, I wouldn't have to urinate on them. He's so immature.

WEDNESDAY, DECEMBER 15, 2010

Got me and my bro Joe Satriani tix as an early Christmas present for tomorrow night at the Fillmore. Was so pumped, blarin' "Summer Song" in the car at lunch. Satriani rocks so hard. Then I called Al with the good news. Al said, "Bro, I can't just take off like that. I got a holiday party I have to go to." Made me so hot under the collar. Asked him, "Is JOE SATRIANI gonna be at this holiday party?!" He wouldn't budge 'cause he promised his wife. Those tickets were 83 bucks apiece! Promises don't cost anything. Decided to go to Paddy's to cool off and figure it out over a few $3 Long Islands.

Couldn't let Dave know about the tickets. He'd gross out the concert chicks. Tried to hint to Carly the bartender that I had an extra ticket. At first I don't think she believed me. Satriani tix are pretty tough to come by. Musta took down six Long Islands workin' up the courage to ask her to go. 'Cause man, with a babe like that on my arm, people'd freak out. Kinda screwed up in the end though. Asked her if she knew anyone that'd want to go. She said, "Oh, me and my friend super would!" Was kinda drunk and just gave 'em to her. Said, "Ho ho ho. Merry Christmas!" So stupid.

THURSDAY, DECEMBER 16, 2010

Can't believe I gave Carly those tix. I guess I'm just too nice and get taken advantage of sometimes. Felt kinda down this morning, but I thought about it, and just givin' away 166 big ones shows that I'm kind of a big spender. Can't really hurt my chances for some action with Carly down the line.

FRIDAY, DECEMBER 17, 2010

The work holiday party starts at 4. Super pumped. Guess there's gonna be drinks and apps and everything. I snuck a peek in the fridge. There's even SHRIMP. Definitely gotta be first in line for the spread so I can get dibs on those shrimp. They always go fast. Saw there's Absolut vodka too. That's the good stuff. Gonna get goin' on the booze early for some stiff ones. When there's free Absolut, you gotta take advantage.

SATURDAY, DECEMBER 18, 2010

Think I did some stuff I shouldn't have at the holiday party. Last thing I remember is hearin', "Look at Shamu over there hoggin' all the shrimp." Got kinda steamed and poured a Solo cup of Absolut on the rocks. It's not hoggin' if it's free! Plus, I needed the shrimp to soak up all the Absolut. It's all about balance. People don't know how to live. It was a holiday PARTY, not a holiday SNOOZEFEST.

I keep gettin' weird emails from co-workers. I guess we went out for drinks after the party to a bar with karaoke and I sang "Me So Horny" with my shirt off. I don't even know that song. Some people took pictures. Kill me.

MONDAY, DECEMBER 20, 2010

Tried to keep it low-key at work today. Mostly just hung out in the bathroom. It was actually pretty great. A couple people called me "2 Live Karl," which I guess is an upgrade from "The Clogger," "Shamu," or "Fatso the Snowman." I kinda like it.

TUESDAY, DECEMBER 21, 2010

Startin' to get super pumped for Christmas. Really need to get shopping. Ol' Santa Karl likes to do it up big and generous.

I forgot about one of my daughter's ballet recitals tonight. Again. Ann is really steamed. Ann called nine times leavin' messages about my kid cryin' and how I was a bad father. Never picked up. Gave Ann a taste of what it's like when someone doesn't pick up the phone. Plus, you gotta play hard-to-get sometimes. I know a thing or two about women.

WEDNESDAY, DECEMBER 22, 2010

Ann called again this morning and said she doesn't know "if it's a good idea" for me to see the kids on Christmas. See, I know women. Give 'em some space, and they'll come runnin'.

All part of the game.

Just remembered that tomorrow is Secret Santa day at work. We drew names at the holiday party and I forgot who mine was 'cause I was bombed. Looks like the 3D Eiffel Tower jigsaw puzzle Ann's mom gave me last year is gonna have to be the gift that keeps on sucking.

Ann's mom's never liked me. Guess I was always too much of a bad boy. When we first started dating in high school, my hair was longer, and her mom would call me "Meathead." So rude. Still calls me that sometimes. And me and Ann would NEVER have alone time. Must have been frustrating for Ann 'cause I know she craved my touch.

When we got married, I don't think she smiled in even one of the pictures. I guess her mom always thought Ann could do better. I know that 'cause I overheard her saying it loud enough for me to hear while I was opening that crappy jigsaw puzzle last year.

THURSDAY, DECEMBER 23, 2010

Just did Secret Santa. Got a sweet Detroit Red Wings scarf! Left the stupid puzzle under the tree and went to eat cookies in the john. They'll figure out who gets disappointed by process of elimination.

No work tomorrow! Gonna head out tonight and get bombed. Show off my new scarf. Babes dig scarves. Shows a lotta class.

FRIDAY, DECEMBER 24, 2010

Woke up late today. Hit RadioShack for some last-minute gifts. My son wanted some stupid Mickey Mouse game, but I got him a RC monster truck instead. And Ann says I'm a bad father. When it comes to Christmas, I got the skills to make the thrills.

Never heard from Ann today. Guess we'll just hook up tomorrow. Me and Dave are pretty trashed on my famous 'nog anyway. Polished off two batches, now we're gettin' into some Crown-and-Diet. Dave said he's gonna call up some gals. This might be the best Christmas Eve I can remember. Really doin' it up jolly!

Crap, where'd I put Ann's heart pendant?! Crap, crap, crap! One more Crown-and-Diet, then I'll look. They're goin' down SO smooth.

The babes never showed up last night. Dave said, "There was a mix-up with who I was." I don't even know what that means. They were probably barf city anyway. Dave has no taste in gals.

Just got back from Ann's. Knew she'd be achin' to see me so I just cruised over. I found her heart pendant under a Wendy's bag in the Sebring on the way there so everything worked out. When I gave it to her, she said, "Karl, you went to Jared!" and laughed a little. She stopped when I told her it was from Zales. Showed her the receipt to let her know I was serious. I do it right. Think she really caught my drift. Plus, I wore a holiday portion of my Tim McGraw cologne. Ann probably woulda been all over me if her folks weren't there. Her mom kept makin' cracks and givin' me the stink-eye every time I'd refill my cocktail. I told her to mind her own business. It felt really good to stand up for myself.

I knew I wasn't gonna get any action from Ann, so I gave the kids their crap, broke the toilet with a monster BM, blamed it on her mom, grabbed a plate of lefties, and split. Feelin' so good right now. Time to relax. Gonna make up another batch of my famous 'nog.

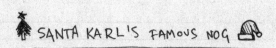

🎄 SANTA KARL'S FAMOUS NOG 🔔

Start by dumpin' a jug of Nog (plain) in a big bowl. Can be Kroger store brand, but somethin' premium like Guernsey really shows you care. Add in 3 boozes, (lots) chef's choice*, like whiskey, rums, or bourbon. Mix it up and serve chilled, topped with NUTMEG.

* NOT Gin. Seems cool, but not.

SUNDAY, DECEMBER 26, 2010

Woke up this morning excited to get into the plate of lefties Ann made me. Saw Dave ate it all. He said, "I thought it was for me?!" Nothing's EVER been for you, Dave. Decided to hit up Paddy's for $1.50 domestics. Told Dave I was goin' to buy toilet paper. He was gettin' on my last nerve. Sometimes I feel like I should bring Dave around more often, but he just doesn't have much class. Always creeps out the foxy chicks.

Had a heckuva time at Paddy's. The best thing about $1.50 pints is that you can pretty much drink as many as you want. Musta had a million, then took down an Irish Nacho to soak it up for the drive home. There was a new gal workin' at Paddy's tonight named Kristen or Carrie or something. Had a super righteous bod and was a real sweetheart. Wanted to chat her up, friendship style, but I was a little bombed. Plus, I spilled a big glob of sour cream on my shirt and didn't want her to think I was a slob right off the bat.

MONDAY, DECEMBER 27, 2010

I found an old Tina's Burrito in the back of the freezer behind the ice trays tonight. Decided to fix it up "supreme" style with all the trimmings: extra cheese on top, salsa, ranch. Really do it up right. Then I heard Dave comin' in the door and didn't want to share so I shoveled it in straight outta the microwave. Stomach hurts really bad now and my tongue hurts almost worse. It was like a thousand degrees. Drank some ranch for a cool-down but it didn't work. I took a couple Pepcid AC and it didn't do anything for my guts either. Stupid Dave, makin' me rush my chow. This is his fault.

TUESDAY, DECEMBER 28, 2010

As soon as I walked in the door tonight, Dave asked me if I wanted to "have a fartin' contest." He was probably holdin' 'em in all day so he'd have the advantage. I don't know how much longer I can live here. Dave's such a grossout.

Had a nice long sit-down in the john tonight. Did some serious thinkin'. I'm gonna really try to make it work with Ann. Dave's just been bringin' me down lately.

WEDNESDAY, DECEMBER 29, 2010

Had to take advantage of Wing Wednesday. Might be makin' some New Year's resolutions, so now is the time to go all out. I took down 18 wings, 2 pitchers, and a cheese fries. So good. Kinda been over-doin' it for the holidays, but that's what they're for. Guess I gotta make a decision whether I go on a diet or just use the gift certificate Ann got me for Casual Male XL. She probably just noticed how I've been beefin' up in the arms department. It's pretty obvious. Actually pretty thoughtful of her. Plus, we both agreed to NOT get gifts for each other, and then we did. Maybe our fire still has some hot coals?

THURSDAY, DECEMBER 30, 2010

Super close to the big NYE bash! So pumped. It's the last hurrah before I really get my program together. Gotta make it count.

FRIDAY, DECEMBER 31, 2010–NEW YEAR'S EVE

Woke up this morning and did a bunch of push-ups so I look jacked later. Gonna check out the band Crush at Wild Spurs country bar next to Paddy's. Seen 'em before. They rock! So pumped. I even picked up a new pair of black jeans. They're kinda tight, but it IS a rock show. They actually look pretty cool.

Dave asked if I wanted to hang with his mom later 'cause she'll have "free pizza and everything." No, loser, I don't. I'm gonna rock out 'til the break of dawn. Hope there's some babes out tonight. Who am I kidding? OF COURSE there will be. Gonna pound a few of my famous Vernors, Hot Damn, and Jim Beam (special recipe). Gotta get a solid buzz goin' before headin' out.

New Year's 2010! Let's do this!

Or is it New Year's 2011? Can never remember. Whatever. Have a blast, you guys!

☆ FROM THE KITCHEN OF KARL WELZEIN ☆ KARL'S FAMOUS VERNOR'S, HOT DAMN, & JIM BEAM. TRADEMARKED!

1. FILL GLASS WITH ICE. MAKE SURE IT'S TALL.
2. ADD IN ONE SHOT OF HOT DAMN.
3. 2-3 SHOTS OF JIM BEAM.
4. TOP WITH VERNOR'S GINGER ALE. NOT CANADA DRY. CANADA DRY WILL RUIN IT AND GROSS OUT YOUR GUESTS. ONE TIME ANN GOT CANADA DRY 'CAUSE IT WAS ON SALE. GOT SO STEAMED.
5. TOAST THE HOLIDAYS WITH GOOD FRIENDS.

SATURDAY, JANUARY 1, 2011

Just woke up at 3 p.m. Tryin' to put the pieces together. Can't find my sport coat. T-shirt was on inside out, the other side was covered in mayo. Crush really rocked it. I even remember dirty dancin' with a few gals. Like four of 'em! I was all over the floor. Two of the gals were grossouts, but I didn't want to be rude. One of the grossouts was all over me and even tried to follow me into the restroom. I told her, "Beat it, I have to crap." Ha! It mighta been the best NYE ever. This year could really be my time to shine.

SUNDAY, JANUARY 2, 2011

Figured out the mayo mystery. Turns out it was ranch. I know because we're out of ranch and we used to have a full bottle. Kinda concerning. Mighta drank a whole bottle of ranch. Oh well. It WAS New Year's Eve.

Really bummin' about Monday tomorrow, you guys. I had big plans to make Pizza Rolls, but there was no ranch, so there was no point. Pizza Rolls without ranch is, well, like Pizza Rolls without ranch. Decided to just go to Wendy's. After four Jr. Bacons, a chili, a large fry, some nuggets, and a Frosty, I stopped at Paddy's. Kinda got a little out of hand there drinkin' Crown-and-Diets to help me digest. Had to pull over on the side of the road after for a quick snooze.

When I got home, I saw that Dave dropped the TV remote in the toilet and just left it there. Who brings the TV remote in the bathroom? That's where we crap. Dave might be the biggest grossout ever. He doesn't know anything about health and hygiene. So friggin' sick of this.

Decided I'm gonna start Atkins tomorrow. It's time to make a change. Life's just gotten so complicated lately. Gonna have one last pig-out on Hormel Chili and some stale taco shells I just found, then hit the sack.

MONDAY, JANUARY 3, 2011–ATKINS DIET, DAY 1

Lunch: Had three Beef 'n Cheddars from Arby's, no buns. Forgot a fork, so they were messy, but delish! Picked up lunch for Ken and some of his curly fries fell out in the bag. Had MAYBE four of 'em. (Bag fries don't count.) I'll behave better at supper. Feelin' good.

Supper: Had a whole pack of beef bologna. Atkins rocks! Dave thinks I'm crazy. Idiot. He doesn't know anything about gettin' slim and trim.

TUESDAY, JANUARY 4, 2011–ATKINS DIET, DAY 2

Kinda screwed up at breakfast. Ate a can of corned beef hash but forgot about the potatoes. Tried to eat around as many as I could. Made up for the potatoes at lunch. Had six Jr. Bacons from Wendy's. They're hardly nothing without the bun. Someone should do something about that. Was still hungry so I got a chili roadie. Then I had a biggie spill in the Sebring.

WEDNESDAY, JANUARY 5, 2011–ATKINS DIET, DAY 3

Lunch: Wing Wednesday was built for the Atkins Diet. Took down 24 wings at BW3's. NO waffle fries was so hard, but I did it. Proud of myself.

Supper: Two $5 Hot-N-Ready Little Caesars pizzas (ate the cheese and pepperoni only). Sold Dave the crusts for $3. Idiot. I would've given him the crusts for just a buck.

Snack: Sucked the cheese off some Cheetos. Kinda better than eating 'em. Think I invented a new diet thing?

Woke up so thirsty. Dave drank the water I keep in an old orange juice bottle in the fridge so it's cold and fresh with just a hint of orange. Tap water is disgusting. Super P.O.'d. Drank half a two-liter of flat Pepsi instead. I know it's not Atkins, but I can't be perfect when there're circumstances beyond my control. I'll make up for it tomorrow.

THURSDAY, JANUARY 6, 2011—ATKINS DIET, DAY 4

Really lookin' forward to the weekend, you guys.

Lunch: Spent 20 minutes at Subway convincing the guy to make me a meatball sub without any bread. Why is that so hard? Also, don't ask me if I want chips when I'm not supposed to have chips. It's really insensitive. This guy is just a jerk, I guess. I probably won't go back.

Plus, he wrapped it all weird and the sauce leaked out on the car seat. I should take the cleaning bill to the manager. Maybe get a free sub?

Supper: Ate a whole summer sausage. Dave made a bunch of cracks. He's such a loser. Doesn't he get that everyone's cool with the gays now? And I'm super not gay. Ask ANY babe.

FRIDAY, JANUARY 7, 2011—ATKINS DIET, DAY 5

Lunch: Had five Coney dogs from Leo's. No bun. Forgot a fork again so they were kinda messy to eat in the car. Chili, cheese, and mustard everywhere. This shirt has seen its last Friday. Gotta get a fresh one for after work. Supposed to meet my bro Al for supper and drinks later. Look out, Chili's, the Welzein boys are comin'!

Supper: Had just an ok time at Chili's with Al. They wouldn't make an Awesome Blossom without any breading for my diet. I hated to make a stink, but the customer is always right. I'm not some jerk, I'm just a guy tryin' to get in shape. I got the chicken fajitas for my entrée. Took the tortillas to go. Gonna sell those to Dave.

We coulda had a fun time, but Al brought his wife Toni. She kept askin' why I don't ever see my kids. Toni sucks sometimes. That's why I try to only keep it bro-to-bro with Al. Toni kept callin' me Jack LaLanne 'cause of my diet. Like I'm some old grossout weirdo. She even brought up Ann a bunch. Me and Ann are FINE, thank you very much. Might be better than ever. I think Toni might be jealous that I'm gettin' in shape and Al's not. AND she kept sayin' how beer isn't Atkins. #1: They were Michelob Ultras, and #2: It's ALMOST my cheat day. If I cut it short tomorrow, it'll even out.

Got a 12-pack of Ultras on the way home. Goin' down so smooth. SO. Smooth. I hate bein' judged. Like Al's better than me. Sick of this.

I don't get to see Al as much as I'd like to anymore. He doesn't live real close. But when we were kids, man, we were unstoppable. If you messed with one of us, then you got what was comin' to you, tag team style. One time, the older paperboy named Sean put a rock in a snowball and threw it at my face. Cut my cheek real bad. So the next morning me and Al went down to the corner where his delivery batch got dropped off and took a whizz all over most of it. Then we threw the rest of his papers in the middle of the road. Ha!

We were always lookin' out for each other like that. Had to. Our dad was never around and after a while he just kinda disappeared. Whenever we asked about him, Mom just said, "He was in a snowmobile accident" and she "didn't want to talk about it."

As we got older, we figured our dad just took off. Always kinda hurt. Then, after our mom passed away, me and Al found a newspaper clipping in her stuff of some guy that was on a snowmobile at night when his neck hit a support wire for a telephone pole. Took his noggin' off. The guy in the article had a different name though. I think Mom just wanted it to be our dad and figured it was as good a story as any.

SATURDAY, JANUARY 8, 2011—ATKINS DIET, DAY 6

Cheat day rocks! Had a big pancake breakfast, then headed over to Paddy's. Felt good because I really earned it. Had such a blast. I started with a double order of Crispy Potato Skins, then moved right on into the Paddy Melt with a side of the sweet potato fries. Boy, those are tasty. Felt like the first time I ever had 'em. After a few cold brews and a couple restroom trips, I got geared up again and went for the Chicken Ranch Pizza (XL). It was just like old times. They use RANCH as the sauce. It's so incredible. AND that goes with my diet, so I was still makin' an effort on my cheat day. Must have five lbs. of leftovers. Was supposed to cut cheat day short, but it's wrong to waste food, and it's stupid to give it to Dave. I'm just gonna try to eat it as fast as possible to make the deadline, then get back on track. Gotta finish this 12-pack too. Man, feels good to put in a solid effort and really commit.

SUNDAY, JANUARY 9, 2011—ATKINS DIET, DAY 7

Kinda overdid it for cheat day, but I'm back on the horse again. "I'm a diet cowboy, on Aaaaatkins I ride!"

Makin' cheese Steak-umms and brats for the Philly vs. Green Bay game (no buns). Maybe invite Ann. She loves Karl's Steak-umms (special recipe with my secret herbs and spices).

MONDAY, JANUARY 10, 2011—ATKINS DIET, DAY 8

Lunch: Ate a crapload of KFC but took the coating off. It's worse than you can imagine. That coating is there for a reason. Ann finally texted me back about yesterday though. She said, "Thanks for the invite, sorry I didn't get back to you! Maybe another time." Playin' hard-to-get. She misses me big time.

Supper: Gonna kill off the rest of these Steak-umms and hit the sack. Monday, see ya later, sucker.

TUESDAY, JANUARY 11, 2011—ATKINS DIET, DAY 9

Had a rough day. Went to work with some Just For Men smeared on my cheek. I lied and said it was cigarette ashes. The nosey office lady said, "You should try to quit, Smokey the Bear." I hate her guts. Made me SUPER P.O.'d. Think the diet's getting to me. I'm usually a cool customer about the insults. Might be crabby too 'cause they bought us Panera Bread for lunch today. Soup without the bread bowl part is just a rip-off. And it wasn't very sensitive to my dietary needs to get Panera BREAD when they KNOW I can't have BREAD. It's almost like they did it on purpose. I love their sourdough but stayed strong. It was really hard not to cave in.

When I got home, Dave found the box from my Just For Men in the trash. Still won't shut up about it. Thinks it's home perm for guys or some crap. Dave's so friggin' jealous it makes me sick. I'M gettin' slim. I'M lookin' good. And he's a lonely pig. I'm gonna eat some salami and cheese over the sink in the kitchen and hit the sack. Screw Dave. Stupid a-hole.

WEDNESDAY, JANUARY 12, 2011—ATKINS DIET, DAY 10

I bought a chin-up bar on the way home from work. Dave already hung a wet towel on it 15 minutes after I put it up. Don't even know where he got it. He didn't shower or anything. Now Dave's crackin' up 'cause I can barely do one and a half of 'em. Like he should talk. I'm probably just sore from doin' push-ups in the john at work. Gonna make a no-bread hot roast beef sandwich and gravy for some energy, then give it another go. Dave better shut his mouth.

THURSDAY, JANUARY 13, 2011-ATKINS DIET, DAY 11

Really lookin' forward to the weekend, you guys. Had a nice sit-down lunch today at Big Boy. Had the Super Big Boy, no bun. The no-bun thing really lets the taste shine through. My arms were pretty sore from chin-ups so I had to eat it all hunched over. The cute waitress asked if I was ok. Told her I was sore from training. She kind of gave me a look up and down. I felt like a real piece of man meat. It was awesome! I'm really doin' it. Might stop at Paddy's on the way home for a few well-earned cold ones.

FRIDAY, JANUARY 14, 2011-ATKINS DIET, DAY 12

Fell back asleep on the couch this morning and was three hours late for work. Gave the ol' "diarrhea" excuse and went straight to lunch. Got Taco Bell. Two hard shells and four soft shells. Only ate the filling though. They should have an Atkins menu for those with special needs.

Ann called. Not for a good reason though. I guess the Carlsons want to have us over to see if they can help us with our "problems." Why is Ann all gung ho to meet up with them to talk, but I can't get any one-on-one time? I can't work my moves in front of those idiots.

Great, just thinkin' about havin' to see the Carlsons gave me real diarrhea. That or the Taco Bell. More likely the Carlsons. I gotta relax. Gonna see if Dave wants to meet at Chili's after work.

SATURDAY, JANUARY 15, 2011-ATKINS DIET, DAY 13

Got a little out of control at Chili's last night with Dave. Stupid Carlsons had me so stressed. Musta had eight margs. I know they're not on my diet, but I needed to relax. Mental health is important too. Left the Sebring at Chili's and had Dave drive home. I threw up pretty bad in Dave's Skylark. He just wiped it up with an Arby's bag and wasn't P.O.'d or anything. I give him a hard time, but he's a pal. Dave said he's worried about me fixin' things with Ann. Had some good points. Would Ann let me throw up in her car and not get mad about it? Bet not.

I'm supposed to meet up with Ann at the Carlsons at 6. Head's pounding. Dave brought home like 17 dollars worth of Taco Bell though, so it's gettin' me back on my feet. Forgot how good the shells are. Diet cheat day is best when you've earned it. Gonna pound some Michelob Ultras to get loose and conversational and head over. Dave thinks I should tell the Carlsons to shove it. Ha! We're kinda havin' a blast.

9:45 P.M.

Just got back from the Carlsons. Tina made the WORST sloppy joes I've ever had. Who screws up Manwich? Idiot. She said she adds her own herbs and spices to "make 'em gourmet." Tina must think "gourmet" means "rotten horse meat" in French. They were so disgusting I could barely eat two of 'em. Took four Crown-and-Diets to wash 'em down. She should call 'em "Pukey Tinas."

After supper we had a sit-down in the living room WITH THE TV OFF. So awkward. Plus, I had the tummy rumbles from the Pukey Tinas. Doug made some crack about my T-shirt bein' "tighter than a witch's butthole." I whispered to Ann, "Oh, like Tina's?" She almost spit. Then they tried to start in with all this counseling mumbo jumbo. Gave us some stupid books. Like you can just read your problems away. Ann was a real sweetheart though. Even touched my hand once. Man, I sure miss that touch. I could tell she even thought they were bein' stupid. I went to get a refill and she said, "Make me a double." You go, Ann!

Tina made some comment 'bout me "lookin' pretty rough." Ann said, "He looks just fine, Tina. If anything, Doug could take some cues from Karl." Doug got up and left the room! I almost had a heart attack, it was so awesome. When we left, I walked Ann to her car. She thanked me for comin' and said it "really meant a lot" to her. Felt like old times. Even got a peck on the lips!

Dave thinks it all sounds like a load and I should just let her go. We're takin' down a case of Labatts and hashin' it out. Great weekend, you guys. Great. Friggin'. Weekend.

SUNDAY, JANUARY 16, 2011—ATKINS DIET, DAY 14

Dave made Bloodies for the Bears game. Remember that old SNL skit? "Ditka. Sausage. Bearsss." Ha! I was crackin' him up. Least I could do. Bloody Marys are pretty much like a meal you eat all day and they're perfect for my diet. Pretty thoughtful of Dave. He was makin' those bad boys STRONG too. Ran out of vodka and had to start makin' 'em with tequila. Man, we were gettin' ROWDY. Dave tried to do some chin-ups and yanked the bar outta the door frame. Made the biggest crash on the floor ever. HAHAHAHAHA-HAHAHA! Oh man, he was rollin' around on the ground yellin', "Oh my God my back my back!" So friggin' funny. I couldn't stop laughing. When he landed on the ground, it sounded like someone dropped an elephant out of an airplane. He even wanted to go to the hospital. I called Ann and we had a good laugh. Man, I miss that laugh. I was so pumped, I pounded a batch of margs, then it was time for a snooze.

After I woke up, Dave was hoggin' the whole couch with a bag of frozen chicken tenders on his bare back. MY chicken tenders.

MONDAY, JANUARY 17, 2011-ATKINS DIET, DAY 15

Lunch: Had a BIG healthy Greek salad and two Coney dogs (no bun) from Leo's for lunch today. Felt good to start the week off right. Didn't get enough dressing for my salad though. Rule of dressing is, you should always get enough so you can't SEE the salad. Gotta remember to ask for extra next time, even though I shouldn't have to.

They let us out early today for MLK Day. Dave took the day off 'cause his back is "killing" him. When I got home, he started in with the complaining and askin' for favors. Really selfish. MLK Day isn't about YOU, Dave. Had to get outta there so I went to Chili's for several cocktails. Also had the Grilled BBQ Chicken Salad, which added up to two salads for the day. Double health. On the way home I drove by Ann's a few times. I thought about stopping by, but I had too many cocktails.

Just got home, made a salami snack, and crashed a few plates. Dave told me to keep it down. He's still bitchin' about his back. It's borrrrring. Dave's back problem is borrrrring. You're borrrrring, Dave. Boring boring boring. Wanna call Ann but it's too late to call Ann. Kinda bombed. You know what, this was a great day for a great man. Gonna go drink a beer in the car and rock some smooth soul R&B 'cause Dave is a boring wuss and MLK is the man. Gotta take advantage of the rights he died for us for.

TUESDAY, JANUARY 18, 2011-ATKINS DIET, DAY 16

This morning, Dave actually said that because I installed the chin-up bar, his back injury is kinda my fault. Oh, I suppose it's my fault he's a big fatso too? He's just trying to make me feel bad and wants me to drive him to Urgent Care. You don't drive with your back, idiot. If he really needs to go, he can drive himself.

Lunch: Got YaYa's. Half chicken and coleslaw. Tried to keep it light 'cause of the MLK Day cocktails.

Ann called. She wants to know if I want to come over and help with my daughter's school project. Of course I don't want to, but I'm going to anyway. It'll get me out of hearin' Dave piss and moan about his back. Plus, it'll remind Ann how ol' Karl knows a thing or two about school projects.

WEDNESDAY, JANUARY 19, 2011-ATKINS DIET, DAY 17

Think I really wowed Ann with my help on the science project. I did some sweet cutouts of the planetary system. Cutouts are my specialty. It's kinda awkward with my son though. He wouldn't even come out of his room to say hi. My daughters kept calling me "Karl." Thought that was pretty cool. Couldn't put any moves on Ann with the kids in the way though. But on the way out I winked and asked her for a "rain check." She caught my drift. It was pretty smooth.

When I got home, Dave had finally got off the couch and went to bed. The cushions reek like his dirty behind now. Had to put down a bunch of paper towels to sit on it. Don't want a contact stink.

Lunch: I took out 18 Spicy Garlics for Wing Wednesday. They kept comin' up on me at work. Had to keep goin' to the john to belch 'cause someone said, "What smells like a rotten garbage disposal?" Blamed it on Ken. Ha!

Ken's pretty much my #1 pal at work. I think he kinda looks up to me as the "renegade" of the operation. He's not really down for bad boy stuff though. We probably couldn't hang outside of the job. Plus, he's always wearin' nice shoes and ties and talkin' about stuff like vacations he went on with his wife. Stuff no one's really interested in. I mean, Ken's cool in the daytime, but I don't know if he could really rock it, after-hours style. I mean, he shaves EVERY day.

THURSDAY, JANUARY 20, 2011–ATKINS DIET, DAY 18
Dave said his mom is comin' to stay with us this weekend. Think he shoulda discussed it with me first. Got so steamed I fell off the wagon and got some Burger King. What the heck am I supposed to do with his mom nosin' around?! I can't even look at him. Takin' up the whole couch. Askin' for crap. Backs don't stay hurt for a whole week. Sick of this. Going to Paddy's.

FRIDAY, JANUARY 21, 2011–ATKINS DIET, DAY 19
Lunch: They got us pizza at work. Ate seven slices, the cheese and pepperoni only, no crust. Got a bunch of "wasteful" comments from Nosey Lady. YOU eat the crust then! I'm on a diet and I can't have crust and if they made pizza without crust I'd get that but they don't so this is how it is, ok! It's not like I don't WANT to eat the crust. I'm making sacrifices to better myself. What are YOU doing, sow?!

Dave said his mom's on the way. Looks like I'll be on my way too, out the door when she gets here. He said, "You gotta stay! She's gonna make supper and everything!" No, Dave. I'm going to Applebee's like an adult.

11:15 P.M.
Had such a blast tonight. Stopped at Wild Spurs for a few after Applebee's. Was in a good mood 'til I saw that Dave's mom was in my bed. So P.O.'d. I just washed those sheets on Wednesday. Now

they're gonna have old-lady smell. She better do laundry before she leaves. Can't believe I have to sleep on the couch. #1: It smells like Dave's farts. #2: I'm a grown man who deserves a bed. #3: This is bullcrap.

Dave's mom got up to see "what the ruckus was." Mind your business and go back to bed! I was makin' hot dog nachos.* Five minutes later she got up to have me turn down the TV. I friggin' live here, you old bag. I worked hard all week. It's Friday. This is MY time. I had to go outside for a smoke to cool off. When I came back in, she was in the john for 20 minutes. Such a nightmare.

SATURDAY, JANUARY 22, 2011–ATKINS DIET, DAY 20
Dave's mom woke me up at friggin' 7:30 a.m. today. "Startin' some breaky for my Dave. How do you like your eggs, Mr. Karl?" I like 'em shut up. Ate my omelet and got the heck outta there for some peace and quiet. Went and sat in my car at Paddy's 'til they opened.

SUNDAY, JANUARY 23, 2011–ATKINS DIET, DAY 21
Had to watch football on the floor like a little kid today 'cause Dave and his mom were hoggin' the couch. Then I bet Dave that if the Bears lost, I'd run around the block with my shirt off. If they won, he had to order a pizza. Supreme.

They lost. Dave said, "Guess the only pepperonis we'll be seein' are yours." Told him I never said WHEN I'd run around the block with my shirt off. Too bad, so sad. It's freezing out. I'm not stupid. His mom said I wasn't being fair. Think she just wanted to see me

---

* 'Chos with hot dogs instead of chips. Captain Karl's Dog 'Chos take all the great toppings of regular 'chos and dump 'em on top of cut-up hot dogs. It's an American-Mexicali healthy protein taste explosion. Your bod'll say, "Gracias, amigo."

with my shirt off. I see her givin' me looks. Then Dave said he didn't care if I don't run around the block with my shirt off 'cause he wasn't gonna buy the pizza anyway. He's such a cheater.

MONDAY, JANUARY 24, 2011-ATKINS DIET, DAY 22

Lunch: Four soft shell supremes. Asked for no shells. Just dump the crap in a wrapper, Taco Bell. Jeez. How hard is that to understand? I'm tryin' to start the week off right and I don't have time to dig around shells.

Dave's mom FINALLY left this morning. Overheard her sayin', "I'm worried about your friend Karl. He seems to be having a hard time." I'M having a hard time?! What about DAVE?! Why don't you judge your own son first, idiot. Good riddance.

Heard Dave's mom give him $40 for us to go out to eat. He better not hog it. Told him we should go out for steaks. He "doesn't know" if he wants steaks. Why should he pick? I'm the one who suffered. And his mom didn't even wash my sheets that she stunk up with old-lady smell. I'm gonna have to sleep on the bare mattress like a drug addict.

Supper: No-bun Steak-umms 'cause stupid Dave won't decide where to spend the $40.

TUESDAY, JANUARY 25, 2011-ATKINS DIET, DAY 23

Dave decided we should spend the $40 on Olive Garden. He knows I can't have pasta or breadsticks. Think he did it on purpose to be a jerk. Still, was super pumped. Free supper is THE best.

OG rocked. I got the Steak Toscano. Forgot they do a nice steak. I let Dave have the Tuscan potatoes. Man, he really put it away. Dave went for the Chicken and Shrimp Carbonara. It sure was a nice-sized portion. Killed me to watch him go to town on it. I made up for it by takin' down two whole serving bowls of the "never-ending salad." Guess they "never" saw me comin'. Ha! I figured I had some carbs saved up, so we went kinda nuts on 20 oz. Bud Lights. They pour 'em real cold at OG. Went down so smooth. The bill was like 80 bucks, and guess who didn't have any more than $40? Dave. Guess who got stuck? Me. Dave said, "But I'm payin' HALF!" THAT half was both of ours. Pretty unfair. We had such a blast though, so I wasn't too P.O.'d. My only real complaint was when the waitress gave me a hard time about takin' home a basket of breadsticks for cheat day. They were already on the table! Couldn't waste 'em.

Felt a little bummed bein' at Olive Garden without Ann. That was one of our special places to celebrate. I gotta work harder on "us."

WEDNESDAY, JANUARY 26, 2011–ATKINS DIET, DAY 24
Lunch: Took down a dozen Caribbean Jerks at B-Dubs for Wing Wednesday. Dipped 'em in half ranch, half blue cheese dressin' (my special concoction).

Got a ton of big plans for the weekend. Asked Ann if she wanted to catch a flick. And I think this cute new gal at work is givin' me vibes. She said, "Excuse me, SWEETIE" today. Ann said, "Sounds good, we'll see," which is, of course, a yes. Think this whole diet and positive attitude is bringin' on the babes. I really feel like everything's coming together. Gonna do some push-ups and eat the insides of a few Hot Pockets. Gotta look GOOD this weekend! Cranked up Van Halen's "Panama." And no, I won't turn it down, Dave. I'm in such a groove right now.

THURSDAY, JANUARY 27, 2011–ATKINS DIET, DAY 25
Shoulder is really hurtin' from the push-ups. Could sure use a rub-down.

Had two Coney dogs for lunch today (no buns). So hard to eat with one hand. Needed the other to ice my sore shoulder. The damn ice bag kept leakin' and soaked my shirt. You could see right through it. Nosey Lady asked me, "What happened? Are you ok?" Told her I hurt my shoulder workin' out. She gave me some weird look. Think my see-through shirt and chafed man pecs were distracting. Went in the john to try and dry my shirt off. Took like 20 minutes. Ken came in and said, "What, you fall in?" Ha! Had to give it to him. Classic burn.

After work I asked Dave where a good place for a massage was. He sent me to some scary Oriental place with bars on the window. No thanks. I know what happens in those places. They get you relaxed in the guy zone, then steal your wallet. Dave has zero street smarts. Just gonna have to make do with a big helping of Icy Hot.

FRIDAY, JANUARY 28, 2011–ATKINS DIET, DAY 26
Got a shoulder wrap with a thermal gel pack in it for my injury. Looks kinda bad boy, like Mad Max. Cute new gal at work gave me a few looks.

In other babe news, Ann got back to me about our movie date. She wants to see *Country Strong* with Tim McGraw. I'm gonna wear my Tim McGraw cologne so it's like 3D. She'll go bonkers. Supposed to meet Dave at Paddy's tonight. Told him just for a few though 'cause of my big date tomorrow. Dave said, "With who? The toilet?" What does that even mean? Such an idiot.

SATURDAY, JANUARY 29, 2011–ATKINS DIET, DAY 27
Had a blast at Paddy's. Dave hit on this one gal and she said, "Gross, dude" right in his face. I laughed so hard. Told Dave his new name is "Gross Dude." Just kills me! "Hey, Gross Dude, get me a fresh beer."

Ha! "P.U.! Who stunk up the can? Oh, musta been my roomie, Gross Dude." Oh man. "Nice stain on your shirt. Is that ranch or mayo, Gross Dude?" Told Dave he should be a superhero named "Gross Dude." He could gross out all the bad guys. Stop that thief, Gross Dude! (Farrrrrrrt.) Man, think Dave is gettin' P.O.'d. Oh, did I say "Dave"? I meant "Gross Dude." HAHAHAHAHA! Can't stop laughing. Can't breathe. GROSS DUDE! Holy shit.

I gotta get ready for my big date with Ann. Just noticed Gross Dude used up all of my Tim McGraw cologne. It's not air freshener! So steamed.

SUNDAY, JANUARY 30, 2011-ATKINS DIET, DAY 28

Had a blast with Ann yesterday. After the movie we went to Damon's for ribs. SO good. Ann ordered the half rack. I told the waitress that "Ann already had a full rack, know what I mean?" I got the full rack ('cause I don't have one, know what I mean?) with a loaded baked potato 'cause it was my cheat day. And of course, we started with the Onion Loaf. If you go to Damon's, the Onion Loaf is a must-have, you guys. Real crowd-pleaser. I stuck with beers, but Ann plowed through a ton of margs. She was gettin' sassy. When I dropped her off at home, we even had a few smooches. I thought about tryin' to go all the way but wanted to be a gentleman. Plus, I had to crap. I mean, I DID feel on her beauties a little over the shirt. I'm only human!

Goin' home to Dave's smelly butt afterward never made me so sad. Can't stop thinkin' 'bout Ann.

MONDAY, JANUARY 31, 2011-ATKINS DIET, DAY 29

Lunch: Got two Quad Steak Burritos from Taco Bell. That's EIGHT helpings of steak. Ate around the shells and rice. It was probably the highlight of my day. Really sick of winter. Wish I could get my boat out.

Supper: Had no-spaghetti spaghetti. Pretty tasty. It's basically Italian chili. Wonder why Italian chili isn't a thing? I might look into getting a patent. Dave said it's a stupid idea. Oh, so sorry for having actual dreams, Dave. He's such a no-nothing asswagon.

Gonna pour me another tall G&T for thinkin' and hash this idea out. "Captain Karl's Italian Chili." Maybe have a little picture with me in a captain's hat on my boat? Could really sweep the nation.

TUESDAY, FEBRUARY 1, 2011–ATKINS DIET, DAY 30

Brought lunch from home today—leftover Italian chili. Didn't appreciate co-workers' comments like "Uh oh, stay away from Karl later." Stupid idiots. Captain Karl's World-Famous Italian Chili doesn't have beans in it. The beans make you toot, not the chili. Hmm, that's a good sales point. "No beans? No problems. So eat up with no worries."

WEDNESDAY, FEBRUARY 2, 2011–ATKINS DIET, DAY 31

Ann called today. One of my daughters got in trouble for "making out" with some boy at recess yesterday. Really steamed. I don't wanna know about that. Trying to block it out. Almost couldn't finish my Wing Wednesday wings. Had a dozen Hot BBQ. Needed to wash 'em down with a couple cold ones to take off the edge. I'd go over there to straighten things out but they let us out of work early 'cause of the snowstorm. Don't wanna waste a half-day on family crap.

I really needed some comfort food, so I took down a large bag of Pizza Rolls. Stomach hurts pretty bad. I shoulda just ate the filling and kept it healthy.

THURSDAY, FEBRUARY 3, 2011-ATKINS DIET, DAY 32

All these stomach problems got me feelin' pretty slim today. Really lookin' forward to the weekend, you guys.

FRIDAY, FEBRUARY 4, 2011-ATKINS DIET, DAY 33

They got us a pizza as a cheer-up for all the rough weather. I took out a whole sausage and 'roni. No crusts. Keepin' my diet on track.

I got to the 'za first so I could make my diet plate and not take any guff for it. Nosey Lady asked me about the missin' toppings. Told her Papa John's musta made a mistake. Guess she actually called to complain. They said it wasn't their fault and now I'm gettin' looks. Sick of this. I wouldn't have to lie if dieting wasn't so looked down at. Plus, lying isn't wrong when it's for the right reasons.

Was chattin' with Ann on the phone and Nosey Lady came by asking about the "weird pizza" like three times. Let it go, loser! I'm talkin' to my babe here. I swear Nosey Lady sounds like a bird with its wings bein' torn off. Finally just told her, "Hope you solve your case, Magnum, P.I." Ha!

Not even sure what Nosey Lady does at work. Think it's some HR made-up crap that's just an excuse to be in my business. How is that a job? It's no one's business when I show up for work, or take breaks, or take the day off, but MINE. I don't need a babysitter. All I know is she dresses like crap, looks like crap, isn't cool, and is the last person that should be tellin' anybody what to do. Maybe if Nosey Lady put more effort into her appearance, she'd get a little more respect. Not from me though, I try not to judge based on "looks." Gotta respect the ladies, you guys.

6

BACK IN THE SADDLE WITH ANN

FEBRUARY 5-27, 2011

SATURDAY, FEBRUARY 5, 2011—ATKINS DIET, DAY 34

Had a blast at Paddy's last night. Gina was bartending and bein' such a sweetheart. If I wasn't tryin' to make it work with Ann, I'd totally make a move. When I came home, I put a pizza in the oven and guess I passed out from too many $2.50, 24 oz. domestic drafts. They were goin' down so smooth. Dave started freakin' out 'cause the pad was all filled with smoke. Like he's never passed out makin' a pizza before.

Dave wants to have a Super Bowl party. Which means he wants ME to have a Super Bowl party. What's he gonna make? Burned toast? 'Course, I do make a mean bratwurst. Johnsonvilles in beer and butter, plus a secret ingredient (special recipe). It's a real crowd-pleaser. Screw it, let's do this! Captain Karl's Super Bowl Party 2011 is a go! (Dave asked to be "first mate." I said no.) Gonna get started on my famous Bloody Karl Mix (special recipe). If you can't handle the heat, stay outta my Bloodies. Ha!

BLOODY KARL'S (HOT)

Take a jug of tomatos juice or V8. V8 is good. Dump out about a glass of it and just throw it away. Useless. Now, start addin' in crap. Tons of Worcestershire. If you think it's too much, it's enough. Maybes some garlic? Def some pickle juice. Black pepper. Take some a three red pepp flake packets from 'za lefties and dump 'em in some Frank's or Tabasco but they're different. But very important is Horseradish. Go bonkers. Buncha scoops. No need to measure anything, just figure it out. Don't be some idiot. Garnish with olives, meats, cheeses, whatever. Shove in a celery stalk and rim the glass with celery salt.

SUNDAY, FEBRUARY 6, 2011-ATKINS DIET,
DAY 35-SUPER BOWL SUNDAY

Dave said he invited a couple friends from work for the Super Bowl party. So, nobody. I hit up a few fellas from the old days and my bro Al. Said they might stop by. Today is gonna rock. Also invited Ann. She might stop by but has plans to go to the Carlsons and told me I was welcome to join. That's like spending Christmas in hell. Tina makes all this "fancy" garbage like hummus and other disgusting crap. I got a full spread goin' here. Made a batch of my Captain Karl's World-Famous Italian Chili, brats are simmerin', made a cheese and sausage plate, chips and onion dip, gonna do a nacho chili dip, Lit'l Smokies in BBQ sauce, Swedish Meatballs a la Karl, and—oh crap! Forgot to start on the Mexican seven-layer dip!

Dave just walked in the kitchen and asked if we're having hummus. First thing out of his mouth. Like he even knows what that is. Hardly anyone does. Think sometimes he just wants to be a show-off.

MONDAY, FEBRUARY 7, 2011-ATKINS DIET, DAY 36

Had a blast for the Super Bowl. Dave destroyed the john right before people were supposed to show up, but I loaded it with Glade and a few candles so we didn't look like animals.

Didn't much care for the Super Bowl music selections. Had those Black Eyed Peas buffoons on. My daughters like that crap, and they hate the Super Bowl. Makes no sense. They shoulda had on Sammy Hagar and the Waboritas. They woulda definitely rocked it. It's what America craves in good ol' USA entertainment. Not some circus crap from a buncha idiots.

Ann stopped by for a drink on her way to the Carlsons. Could tell she didn't want to go. When I pull out all the stops on the eats and booze, it doesn't get any better. Dave actually had a few "work friends" over. 'Course "work friends" aren't REAL friends. Didn't tell him that though. Didn't wanna hurt his feelings. They were pretty cool though. This one Rick guy had a doobie, so we chilled out. And I thought some gal named Sheryl had a pretty rockin' body 'til I woke up this mornin' and she was crashed on the couch lookin' ROUGH. Good thing NOTHING happened between me and her, for the record. The whole pad is kind of a disaster. Guess we got a little outta control. Someone spilled a whole bottle of strawberry daiquiri mix in the carpet. When I got home tonight, Dave hadn't cleaned up anything. I think it was actually worse than when I left this morning. That lardo had the whole day off from the gas station. I did all the work for the party. The least Dave coulda done is cleaned up the mess. He just sat around all day eatin' up the leftover snacks and drinkin' up the extra beers. THERE'S A WHOLE FRIGGIN' BOTTLE OF STRAWBERRY DAIQUIRI SPILLED IN THE MIDDLE OF THE FLOOR! He just put some paper towels over it. I'M certainly not cleaning up. I forked over the cash for the spread. I bought all the booze. Sick of this. Gonna put all the leftover liquor in my trunk. Dave needs to take some lessons in having a little class.

TUESDAY, FEBRUARY 8, 2011–ATKINS DIET, DAY 37

Guess what's not clean yet? The pad. And it's worse, AGAIN. It was bad enough this morning when I stepped on a meatball in the kitchen and had to change my sock. When I got home, there was a half-spilled Doritos bag on the couch. Dave wasn't even home. Who just spills D'reets and leaves? I got a nice buzz on off some of the liquor I had stashed in my trunk and started stewin'. Threw out a bunch of the dirty plates, silverware, and glasses. If Dave can't appreciate things, he shouldn't be allowed to have 'em. The daiquiri-soaked rug? Dumpster.

WEDNESDAY, FEBRUARY 9, 2011–ATKINS DIET, DAY 38

Dave finally came back, said he went to his mom's because the place was "just too disgusting." Clean it then! He's such a baby. Now he's all ticked off 'cause I threw away all that crap. Said I owe him like $200. Like they cost him that much at Goodwill. If anything, he should thank me for at least tidying up a little. I shouldn't have had to do anything at all in the first place. I paid for the whole Super Bowl spread! Besides, I think I did him a favor. He should at least have nice stuff from Target. Show a little class, Dave. Babes dig that. AND that rug was RUINED long before the daiquiri incident. Again, I did him a FAVOR.

Dave won't talk to me. He's just staring at the TV. What is he, a woman or something? If I wanted to be ignored or complained about when I do something nice, I'd get back with Ann.

THURSDAY, FEBRUARY 10, 2011–ATKINS DIET, DAY 39

Really lookin' forward to the weekend, you guys. Dave ate his supper tonight on the bare coffee table. Use a paper towel! What a stupid animal. Then he burned some microwave popcorn real bad. Asked him how long he put it in for. He said, "Dunno, like eight minutes? I like it well done." No one likes that! Idiot. Eight minutes for popcorn? When's your new cooking show, Chef Dave? Someone call Bobby Flay for a throw-down! Ha!

It's so smoky in here. I had to knock the detector off the ceiling with a broom. Now he's trying to choke the popcorn down like it's fine. Oh, this is hilarious, but I can't stand to be in here anymore. Such a stench of stupidity. I'm goin' to my car to make a trunk liquor drink. Already polished off a sixer of talls. Went down so smooth. Thirstday rocks.

2:38 A.M.

Just woke up in the Sebring. Dozed off. So cold. Can't get warm. Gotta hit the sack.

FRIDAY, FEBRUARY 11, 2011—ATKINS DIET, DAY 40

Called Ann to tell her I have somethin' really special planned for Valentine's. Don't know what it is yet, but she said she's in. Super pumped. Might have to head out to Paddy's and cut loose.

1:45 A.M.

Makin' some Lit'l Smokies. Really overdid it at Paddy's. Gina comped me some Jameson shots. Didn't want the last one but did it to be polite. Had to barf it up in the john.

Dave's all crashed out. What a lame sack of crap. It's Friday. I'm tryin' to party here. Gonna crank up some "Small Town." Always gets the waterfalls goin'. It's so good, you guys. Love me some Johnny Cougar. Great, Dave just shouted from his room to "turn it down." Kiss my white butt, loser. I'm crankin' it up!

Don't know if it's a good idea, but I just realized I could be drinkin' my trunk liquor at work. Just a thought.

SATURDAY, FEBRUARY 12, 2011—ATKINS DIET, DAY 41

Was really draggin' today. Had such a blast last night. Put away three Quad Steak Burritos from Taco Bell for lunch to soak it up. Also got two of those burritos with Fritos on 'em. Genius. Whoever invented that is just genius. It was the perfect base for a few Saturday G&Ts to start the night off. They're goin' down so smooth. Might have to head out early. Maybe Wild Spurs? Get down and dirty on the dance floor.

Still tryin' to figure out what to do with Ann for Valentine's. Wish I didn't get her that heart pendant for Christmas. No way I can top that. I wanna take her somewhere really special though. Like a steak house or something.

Holy crap. Out of nowhere, Dave just went in the bathroom and threw up for no reason! Hahahaha!!! So hilarious, you guys. What a great day. Asked him why he did it. Dave said, "Dunno, just felt like it." What an idiot. Now he's eating Toaster Strudels.

SUNDAY, FEBRUARY 13, 2011–ATKINS DIET, DAY 42

My thighs are all sore. Guess I boogied down last night. Don't remember much. Dave said I came home, knocked over the coffee table, put in *Jewel of the Nile*, and woke him up to say how hot Kathleen Turner was. Guess I put a whole box of Pizza Rolls in the microwave and forgot about 'em. It's a disgusting mess. Dave asked if he could have 'em. Jeez. I gotta go lay down.

11:28 P.M.

Just woke up. Really crashed out there. I'm wide-awake now. Don't know how I'm gonna get back to sleep. Gonna drink a few cold ones and do some push-ups. Gotta burn off some energy. Really shouldn't have taken that nine-hour nap.

1:30 A.M.

Gonna watch some *Becker*. Should do the trick.

3:05 A.M.

Just can't sleep! Still awake. Gonna smoke some of Dave's grass stash. It's supposed to be for special occasions, but I gotta be sharp for V-Day with Ann.

MONDAY, FEBRUARY 14, 2011-ATKINS DIET, DAY 43-VALENTINE'S DAY

Was super late for work today. Like three hours. No one even said anything. Why do I come in on time ever?

Got so much to do for V-Day. Just called Red Lobster and we can't get in 'til like 10:30! Might check out Olive Garden, but Red Lob is kinda the move for action. Olive Garden is more of a place for just huggin'. Also, I have to run to Kohl's for more Tim McGraw cologne. Need a new shirt anyway. Valentine's Day is such a hassle.

At least I nailed it in the gift department. Bam. This is a home run:

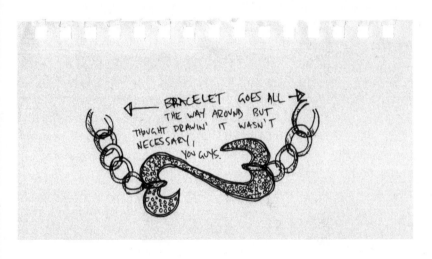

Plus, Jane Seymour designed it. And Ann used to LOVE *Dr. Quinn, Medicine Woman*. Ann has terrible taste in TV shows, but it's really thoughtful of Dr. Quinn to help me out here.

TUESDAY, FEBRUARY 15, 2011-ATKINS DIET, DAY 44

Had such a blast with Ann last night, you guys. Waited until 10:45 to get into Red Lob, but it was WELL worth it. I had the Ultimate

Feast. My go-to at Red Lob. Ann had the Maple-Glazed Salmon and Shrimp. She's watchin' her weight and looks GOOD. And the Cheddar Bay Biscuits? Oh man, they're just the best. I musta had a dozen. I had to take the day off from my diet (special occasion). Seriously, you guys, if you want to crank the romance up, Red Lob knocks it outta the park. Plus, the booze is top-notch and the Berry Mango Daiquiris were goin' down so smooth.

Afterward, we went back to Ann's and watched *Valentine's Day*, Ann's fave, which sucked but, combined with the the daiqs and some red wine, made for a cozy situation. I'm a gentleman, but I'm not gonna say some hanky-panky DIDN'T happen.

Ok, what happened was, we started to go all the way, but then one of my daughter's got up to use the john, so I had to split. Man, it was sure hard to drive home. Ha! Sorry, that was gross. I'm just excited. AND I forgot to give Ann the Jane Seymour bracelet. Didn't even need to! Takin' it back to Kay tomorrow. Double score. Me and Ann talked this morning, about our love being rekindled, and she thinks maybe I should move back in at the end of the month! I'm super pumped, you guys. Dave's been gettin' on my nerves more than ever, so timing couldn't be better. Still, don't know how I'm gonna tell Dave. He'll be so bummed without his partner in crime, Captain Karl. I'm kinda the cool one of the group.

WEDNESDAY, FEBRUARY 16, 2011–ATKINS DIET, DAY 45

Just don't know how to tell Dave I'm hittin' the bricks. We're kinda bros, you know? Maybe tomorrow. I got us a $5 Hot-N-Ready 'cause I feel bad. Even let him have my crust. I only ate the cheese and 'roni. Gotta keep my bod tight for Ann.

Dave just told me how he "used to know a bunch of rockers, but they're all burned out and toasted now. Glad I live the simple life."

I asked him what "rockers" he knew. Dave said, "Dunno, that Don guy from Flint?" Who the heck is "that Don guy"?! Hoo boy, I'm dyin' here. Yeah, I can't tell Dave tonight. We're havin' a blast. That, and he bought the brews. Hate for him to get P.O.'d and hog 'em all for himself.

THURSDAY, FEBRUARY 17, 2011-ATKINS DIET, DAY 46
Dave got d-runk last night. Told me a bunch of weird crap. Like, "I ever tell you I had the biggest one in 8th grade gym class? No lie." Who remembers everyone's peener size from 8th grade? Still, pretty hilarious.

FRIDAY, FEBRUARY 18, 2011-ATKINS DIET, DAY 47
Decided to surprise Dave by firin' up the Weber on the patio for a couple hamburgs and a few brats. Went outside to light the grill and the door locked behind me. Was outside for two hours waitin' for Dave to come home in the 35-degree weather. Had to use up all the charcoal to keep warm. When Dave got home, he said he clicked the lock button on the patio door for "safety." We've NEVER done that. Stupid idiot. I should've been informed. He's lucky I wasn't dead.

After I took a shower to get all the soot off me, I went to the store for more charcoal. While I was gone, it looked like Dave went hog wild on the Michelobs I bought and passed out. Then, when I got the hamburgs and brats cooked, Dave woke up, ate two hamburgs and brat with his hands, didn't say a word, and went back to sleep on the couch. Ever hear of "thank you"? Ass.

Screw Dave. I hid a backup sixer in the veggie drawer, muted the Golf Channel, and cranked up some Allman Brothers. That's all I need, baby.

1:37 A.M.

I miss my boat. I miss my wife. Sick of this crap. Goin' to bed, you guys.

SATURDAY, FEBRUARY 19, 2011–ATKINS DIET, DAY 48

Had a little sunshine peakin' out today. Fired up the grill again for cheat day. Made Captain Karl's Famous Smoke Pork Chop Sammies. This trick is, I put a fried egg ON the pork chop sandwich so the yolk gets all in there with the bread and mm-mmm-mm! It's just a little trick I learned on *Diners, Drive-Ins and Dives*. If you need tips on cutting-edge cuisine, you just gotta check out my man Guy Fieri. When it comes to bold flavors, there isn't really anyone in his league right now. Guy's so off the chain. Also, I picked up one of those Miller Lite Home Draft mini kegs. Didn't know anything could go down so smooth. We're havin' a blast. Supposed to meet up with Ann later though, but only if her mom can watch the kids. Hangin' out with my kids is NOT part of the Saturday plan. Gonna crank up some AC/DC.

4:15 P.M.

Whoa, we plowed through that mini keg. Dave's runnin' out for another one. Havin' such a blast. No way I can tell Dave about moving out today. He'll get the blues. Ann said she's gonna stop by for a quick beer in half an hour. Hope she doesn't mind we're a little trashed. Gonna go clean up the john and stuff. Make everything look natural.

SUNDAY, FEBRUARY 20, 2011–ATKINS DIET, DAY 49

Things got pretty weird last night. Me and Dave were waaaay too drunk. Shouldn't have had Ann over. I tried to make her a pork chop sandwich, put the coals on the grill, and forgot to light 'em for two hours. After I finally lit the coals, I forgot I did, and they burned out. I got super steamed and knocked over the grill. Dave said, "What did you do to my grill?!" I said, "Suck it, retard." Kinda was showin' off for Ann, but I just looked like an insensitive jerk. Ann had a few cocktails by then and tried to smooth over the tension by saying, "So, Dave, I guess you're really gonna miss Karl." Spilled the beans. I had to tell Dave how I'm moving out in about a week. Then he completely flipped out with, "How am I gonna find a new roommate?! You screwed me!"

First off, Dave didn't have a roommate before. Ever. Secondly, I wasn't paying rent. If anything HE was freeloading off ME for the booze and eats I provided.

Before Ann left, she gave me a smooch and then shot Dave a look. After she walked out, Dave said, "Bitch." It was go time. Me and Dave musta screamed at each other for over an hour. Everything came out. What a grossout he is, the TP usage. Everything. I told him he'd be LUCKY to ever score with a babe like Ann. And he better straighten up his act 'cause grossouts like him never go all the way. Dave said I changed. How I used to be cool, but now I'm only about fancy cologne and diets like some flamer. Yeah, sue me for growing up, Dave. I called him a know-nothing slob. He punched a hole in the drywall and stormed off to his mom's. Hope he stays there. Been no sign of him all day. Gonna eat some Funyuns and hit the sack. Can't stick to the diet today. Too stressed.

MONDAY, FEBRUARY 21, 2011–ATKINS DIET, DAY 50
Back in the saddle on my diet. Got an Italian Night Club JJ Unwich from Jimmy John's. No bread, they just wrap everything in lettuce. See, I'm NOT crazy. Really sick of people like Dave and idiots at

work judging me for my diet. If restaurants make things for it, it can't be stupid. My brain isn't a pile of garbage. Why don't pizza places make UnPizzas? They'd clean up. And I wouldn't have to take guff for just eating the toppings. Just throw all the melted cheese and crap and sauce in a box and sell it to me. Not that hard.

Felt good to be up and around early today. Forgot it was President's Day and drove to work. We had it off. Got a bunch of stuff done. Did 20 push-ups AND bought TP. Been no sign of dingleberry Dave either. Guess he's still cryin' to his mom. "Oh, Momma, me and Karl awen't fwiends anymo!" What a baby. Not my problem. I gotta start lookin' out for numero uno more.

Havin' such a great night. Made some UnTacos a la Karl. And I got the tube all to myself. Feel like I could watch TV forever. *Coach* is on. Forgot how incredible this show was. Dauber? Hahahahaha!!! Plus, it's been such a pleasure to use the john without Dave makin' beef sounds outside the door. Nothin' like a quiet BM session.

Screw it, I'm crackin' another cold one. I just gotta say, if anyone's a president, this Bud's for you, you guys.

TUESDAY, FEBRUARY 22, 2011–ATKINS DIET, DAY 51

Was really draggin' today. Stayed up way too late. Spent 45 minutes takin' a toilet nap. Got accused of "leaving work." Going in the john is still being at work. I could be sick or something. It's nobody's business what I do in there.

Dave wasn't here when I got home. That meant I got to do some push-ups with my shirt off and not hear crap about it. It really lets me see the progress on my bod. I suppose I should start thinkin' about packin' up my crap, but I'm too sore from those push-ups. Feelin' jacked. Did two sets of 12!

Still no Dave. I'm watchin' *Armageddon*, eatin' pork rinds, sippin' Crown-and-Diets. It's such a winning combination. Livin' it up, Captain Karl style!

WEDNESDAY, FEBRUARY 23, 2011—ATKINS DIET, DAY 52

Happy Wing Wednesday, you guys. Took down a dozen Hot BBQ and six Spicy Garlic. Had to get in some quality protein after my workout last night. Between my extra long lunch, six or seven bathroom breaks, and a fake "run to Walgreens to pick up my prescription," Wing Wednesday is flyin' by. Feelin' frisky, might head out to Paddy's later. Haven't been by to see the gals in a while. Don't wanna be rude.

Just spoke to Ann about when I should do the big move-in. She said we should have a talk with the kids first. That sounds like the worst. Definitely goin' to Paddy's now. It's $3 Long Islands tonight. Gonna settle in and take advantage of the savings. The freedom trail is ending soon.

12:37 A.M.

Came home pretty bombed on Long Islands. Love when Gina works on Long Island night. Gina makes the best Long Islands. Plus, she's got an incredible rack. Not sayin' that to be creepy, just a friendly comment about Gina. Dave was home from wherever when I got home. He just got up and went to bed. Didn't say anything. Dave's a coward about confrontations. I'm kinda the alpha dog around here. That's just my nature, I guess. Is it too late to make pork chops? Might have to do a little shakin' and bakin'. I add my own spices to make 'em Captain Karl style (special recipe). Makin' me a tall Crown-and-Diet.

2:15 A.M.

Pork chops are done. Dave came out of his room and said, "Whatcha makin'?" Nice try, fair weather fan. I don't think so. Hit the sack, jerk. Dave ain't gettin' none of my chops. He can't just expect us to be pals 'cause he wants something. I'm makin' another drinko.

THURSDAY, FEBRUARY 24, 2011–ATKINS DIET, DAY 53

Woke up on the couch this morning. Pork chops were still sittin' there all cold. Left 'em by the sink. Dave'll still eat 'em like some animal. No need to waste food. Don't think they were fully cooked anyway.

Dave's actually bein' pretty cool tonight. Think it was my gift of the trash chops. Said he'd help me pack on Saturday. We took down a Silver Bullet fridge keg.

Oh man, Dave just tried to do a mini keg stand. Crashed on his neck. Ha! What a fatso. Now Dave's icin' his neck with some of my Pizza Rolls. Well worth it for how hilarious that injury was. I gotta hit the sack.

FRIDAY, FEBRUARY 25, 2011–ATKINS DIET, DAY 54

It's. Time. To. Par-tay!!! Last weekend of freedom, you guys. Picked up a whole bunch of snacks and cold ones on the way home. One last blowout with Dave. Even got some Jack for shots. We got a mean buzz goin' on. Headin' out to Paddy's and Wild Spurs. My bro Al's supposed to meet us. Let's do this!

1:35 A.M.

Me, Al, and Dave just got back from Paddy's. Gonna smoke some wacky on the sly. Gotta do it right. Might even watch *Police Academy 2*. Ha! It's such a classic, and on grass, the laughs are a mile a minute. Dave is SO bombed on kamikaze shots. Gina was pourin' 'em heavy all night long. She knew we were celebrating . . . on Al's tab. Now Al's wearin' a 12-pack box on his head. It's his signature move that lets you know that the party is ON.

I'm gonna go take a whizz off the deck. Ha!

SATURDAY, FEBRUARY 26, 2011–ATKINS DIET, DAY 55
So hungover today. Can hardly sit up. Keep having the spins. Don't think I can pack anything today. I can't help that I'm under the weather. Ann will understand. Goin' to lay down on the john floor.

SUNDAY, FEBRUARY 27, 2011–ATKINS DIET, DAY 56
Sent Dave to Mickey D's. Said I'd buy if he'd fly. Gave him a fifty. Didn't think I should have to explain to bring back change. Idiot. He spent the whole 50 dollars. Says it's "McGroceries." The whole fridge is full. Can hardly stand to look at it. Just ate a 20-piece McNuggets with the coating taken off for health.

Gonna have to hold off on the big move until next week. There were just too many things on my plate to get all packed up and whatnot. My life just feels kinda out of control. I wish I wasn't so popular so I'd have more time to focus on the important stuff. I watched the Oscars tonight. Could really identify with the actors. All those people wanting you to party all the time. It gets hectic, you know? Plus, there were a ton of hot babes at the Oscars. It'd be tough to live the married life. Good thing I never tried acting. It'd be so tough to fight off all the gal fans and still focus on my main squeeze, Ann.

Guess I should try to hit the sack. Feelin' kinda down. I wish Dave was awake so we could have a solid guy-to-guy. Could use a pal right now, even if he's a know-nothing idiot.

7

HOLD ON LOOSELY, BUT DON'T LET GO

FEBRUARY 28-APRIL 22, 2011

MONDAY, FEBRUARY 28, 2011-ATKINS DIET, DAY 57

Brought a big bag of Mickey D's lefties to munch on at work. It's really hard to peel the stale buns off the meat for health though. Makin' such a mess. Seriously, you'd be pretty surprised at how far $50 goes at McDonald's. It's almost shocking. $20's worth really woulda been plenty.

Nosey Lady just walked by me and shook her head like I'm stupid. I should smash this McChicken in her dumb face, but she's not even worth the dollar.

Ann wants me to come over for supper with the kids. And not just tonight. Every night until I move back in. Seems a little excessive. I mean, it'd be cool to have some grub with Ann. But with the kids? They don't like me, so why should I put myself out there?

TUESDAY, MARCH 1, 2011-ATKINS DIET, DAY 58

Dinner last night was just ok. My daughters kept calling me "Karl," my son didn't want to sit next to me, and of course I took some guff for just eating the meat sauce without the pasta. It's not "gross," it's "healthy." Decided to lay down the law. Told my daughters to stop calling me "Karl" and that I was their "Dad." They said, "Real dads live with their kids like regular families." Kinda got me in the ticker. I mean, I haven't been around much lately, but who do they think pays the mortgage? Not Ann's eBay business, that's for sure. And it's not like I don't want to be around. Sure, I could just move back in and carry on the charade like we're the family of the year. But I don't want a charade, I want the real deal. Gotta take it slow. I'm the captain of the family, they gotta trust that I know what's best.

WEDNESDAY, MARCH 2, 2011–ATKINS DIET, DAY 59

Family supper again tonight. I miss Paddy's, where people are nice to me and they have $3 Long Islands. I should just fake diarrhea and bail. And why do my kids hate me so much? If they could only see Captain Karl in action, they'd know how cool I got since I moved out. Maybe I should take the kids to Paddy's for lunch this weekend. Let 'em see how chillin' I am with the peeps there. Could be a step in the right direction to gainin' some real respect.

THURSDAY, MARCH 3, 2011–ATKINS DIET, DAY 60

Finished up supper early last night. Shoveled in my meatloaf and hit the bricks. Said I had some "work" to do. "Work" = $3 Long Islands at Paddy's. Couldn't stand to be there anymore. My son wanted me to play some weird magic card game with him. Whatever happened to baseball cards? This is America, not Weirdoville. Just wish we could bond over something I understand, not something that makes me look stupid.

Kinda got outta control last night. Guess I blacked out. Woke up on the living room floor with no pants on. They must put something special in those Long Islands at Paddy's 'cause I got really messed up on like five or six of 'em. Guess I puked a little in the 'Bring. Had to drive to the car wash this morning with a scarf tied around my mouth and nose. It was pretty nasty. Blamed it on the "dog." I'm just so stressed about things with the fam. Must be why I threw up. Being a good dad doesn't really lend itself to a healthy lifestyle.

Headin' over to Ann and the kids' for supper. Bringin' my son a football. This magician crap needs to stop. He'll get murdered at school.

8:45 P.M.
Gave my son that football. He throws more like a girl than my two daughters do. I'm think I'm gonna do some drinking now.

3:26 A.M.
Just got up to take a whizz. Lights were on in the john and the door's locked. Think Dave passed out on the can. Had to take a leak in an empty Miracle Whip jar. Sick of this. Sick of livin' like an animal. Dave better not be dead on the toilet. It'd ruin my whole weekend.

FRIDAY, MARCH 4, 2011–ATKINS DIET, DAY 61

Just snuck into the work fridge to get some leftover no-crust 'za. Needed a little snack. Peeled off the cold cheese and pepperoni. Made some Captain Karl's Pizza Roll-em-ups. They should sell 'em to dieters. It'd be a huge hit. You know, with a couple more amazing recipe ideas, I think I could open up my own restaurant. That'd be such a blast. "Captain Karl's Pizza Ship." Great name. We'd have Italian Chili, Pork Chop Sandwiches a la Karl, Pizza Roll-em-ups, UnTacos, all the fixins, and the coldest beer in town. Man, I gotta draw up some plans. Feelin' inspired.

Nosey Lady just said we're havin' a last-minute meeting about what happened to the pizza leftovers that were for "everyone." No, "we're" not. I'm leaving. Gonna meet Dave for a couple $2.50, 24 oz. drafts at Paddy's before headin' to Ann's. Gotta tell him 'bout my restaurant idea.

10:24 P.M.

Got a little too buzzed for dinner with Ann and the kids. The brews were ice-cold and goin' down so smooth. Went to dinner anyway. Told my daughters that "Captain Karl is sick of this crap with the name-calling!" Now they're calling me "Tugboat." So sick of this. Ate sloppy joes with no bun and spilled a bunch on my shirt. Ann said, "Rough seas, Captain Karl?" Everyone laughed like she was Elayne Boosler. Then my son tried to put a spell on my shirt to make the stain go away. Told him, "Magic's not real." He freaked out and ran to his room. Ann said, "Everyone's a little too riled up. Maybe you should go and we'll see you later." So I guess I'M the bad guy now. For what? Being honest? SO sorry. I guess all the good dads are liars. So steamed. Plus, they were burnin' me down left and right!

Got some Bacardi on the way home. Gonna make some of my special Paradise Coolers to take the edge off. Dave put on some Buffett. We're really chillin'. This is what Friday's all about. Thing is, I don't really like Jimmy Buffett. Don't know if anyone really does. But the lifestyle he represents is so laid-back and chillin' that it's cool to groove out to. Maybe I should write some island songs? "Paradise Cooler" has a nice ring to it:

Paradise Cooler! Oh yeah, it'll rock you down, not fool ya. And when the babes, oh yeah, the babes (guitar pick slide) come runnin', you'll be crankin' for action with satisfaction, ready for an all-night rendezvous of adult passion, on Paradise Cooler!

1:15 A.M.

Gonna boil some hot dogs. These Paradise Coolers are goin' down so smooth.

1:56 A.M.

Gonna have one more Paradise Cooler and another dog. Then hittin' the sack. Feel like I could party forever, but I gotta hit the sack. Havin' a big day with the kids at Paddy's. Can't wait 'til they see how hard I rock.

SUNDAY, MARCH 6, 2011–ATKINS DIET, DAY 63

Just woke up on the couch. Think I kinda made an ass outta myself last night. Feel like such a jerk.

Cool Dad Day started out good. I let my daughters play some Katy Perry in the Sebring on the way to Paddy's. Have you seen that babe? Holy mackerel. When we got to lunch, my son ordered a chef salad. I told him to get something nice like the Paddy Melt. He wouldn't budge. It was so embarrassing. I told my daughters to get the BLT Pizza. They freaked out because it has ranch for the sauce. Why would that be a BAD thing? All they wanted was fries and ketchup. You could get that anywhere! This is PADDY'S. I did it right with the Irish Nachos. My daughters couldn't understand why they were "Irish." 'Cause they have fries instead of chips, that's why. They thought they should be called "French Fry Nachos." That's BORING. Why are they so damn boring?

I introduced my kids to Gina. One of my daughters asked, "Are you Karl's girlfriend?" Then, "Why does Karl think he's so cool? Do you think Karl's cool? Our mom doesn't think so. Does Karl try to kiss you? Gross. We think Karl likes you." And on and on. I tried to change the subject and ordered a bucket of beers. Gina gave me some weird look and walked away. I felt like such a loser. Then my son started in with the magic wand crap. I went to the john to re-group and when I got back the food was there. One of my daughters said, "We told Gina you were makin' #2 and she should just leave the food because you make #2 a lot."

I shoveled down my Irish Nachos and only pounded five of the six bucket beers 'cause I was drivin' the kids, then got the heck outta there. After I dropped them off, I went back to Paddy's to try and smooth things over with Gina. Didn't want her to think I'm a grossout. Got another bucket of beers. Then a few Crown-and-Diets. Guess I knocked over some things and had to leave. I just wanted to seem cool to my Paddy's peeps. Don't want them to think all Captain Karl is about is takin' craps. Feelin' bummed about it. Like a big, fat crap machine. Kids are just no good for self-esteem.

Had to have supper with the fam AGAIN tonight. Was so hung-over and Ann was this and that and blah blah blah and the kids were blah blah blah. My daughter said how she met "Karl's girl-friend Gina" at Paddy's and how she said I'm a "dump machine" or whatever. Had to explain all of it. So terrible. Then my son kept say-ing our sauerkraut and sausage supper was "cauldron snakes." Sick of this magic crap. Wonder if he's a "special kid"? Kinda concerning. I really need to call a family meeting about all this. Buncha weirdo crap from everyone is NOT gonna fly.

MONDAY, MARCH 7, 2011–ATKINS DIET, DAY 64

Sometimes it feels like it'll be cold forever and I'll never be able to golf or get my boat out again. Makes me wanna run in traffic. This Monday has a little more funk on it than usual. Really draggin', you guys. Ate a variety pack of cold cuts for lunch. So boring.

Supposed to go over to Ann and the kids' for supper in a bit. How is "family time" supposed to be special when it happens every day? It's like, if every *Sports Illustrated* was the swimsuit issue, then that wouldn't be special anymore either. Awesome, but not special. I wonder where mine went anyway? Picked up the new copy at 7-Eleven and didn't even get to look at it. Dave probably snagged it.

TUESDAY, MARCH 8, 2011-ATKINS DIET, DAY 65

Supper was nice last night. My daughters had some sort of practice for something I don't care about and my son was eating at a friend's. Ann made baked BBQ chicken. I passed on the potatoes. She was impressed with how I'm still sticking to my diet. Just ate a ton of chicken. On the way out, I snuck in a little smooch AND got me a squeeze on her caboose. She thought I was being silly. Nope. DEAD serious.

WEDNESDAY, MARCH 9, 2011-ATKINS DIET, DAY 66

Never went to Ann's yesterday. Told her I had to help Dave with some "girl problems." Which really meant lookin' for the missing swimsuit issue. Finally found it in the john. It was under a bunch of my *Men's Health*s. Think I hid it there from Dave. It's a good spot.

Had THE BEST supper with fam tonight: Filet-O-Fishes and Shamrock Shakes. Not part of my diet, but I guess God or whatever says to eat it today. I took down a regular Filet-O-Fish and a Double F-O-F. No fries though. Didn't want to overdo it. My son only had a few bites of his 'cause he only likes chicken tenders dipped in ketchup like some girl. Told him to quit complainin' and change it with "magic." He started to whine and pushed the F-O-F away. Told him, "See, magic's pretend" and ate his too. Nothin' wrong with some tough love.

I gotta confess, I stopped on the way home for another Filet-O-Fish. Didn't want to look like a hog in front of the fam. They just go down so smooth, you guys. Swear to God, I could hit McD's for another F-O-F right now. Gotta use self-control.

Dave asked me if I went to church for Ash Wednesday. No, Dave, I'm an adult. He's still wearing his ashes like some ramrod. I ate Filet-O-Fishes, Dave. It's good enough. Just 'cause you look like someone put out a cig on your face doesn't make you better than me. Also, Dave gave up drinking for Lent. I'd give up something, but I already suffer enough for my diet. God shouldn't be greedy on the suffering. Diets are really hard. I just don't get prayin' and all that stuff. Never did anything for me. I always worked hard for everything on my own. Dave should be careful, you should only pray when you NEED something. Like, when I had that heart attack and crashed into a tree, I prayed a little. But that was different.

THURSDAY, MARCH 10, 2011–ATKINS DIET, DAY 67
Even after all those Filet-O-Fishes, I'm still feelin' pretty slim today. Think Mickey D's fish must be the "good for you" fat like avocado. I could sure go for another Shamrock Shake right now. Fightin' it off, gotta stay strong. They're only for a limited time though. I feel like every day I don't get a Shamrock Shake is a waste and I'll regret it later. Gettin' in healthy shape is so stupid sometimes and can really screw with your life. They should make Diet Shamrock Shakes. They make diet everything else. C'mon, Mickey D's, do it for us health nuts!

Happy Friday to ya, you guys. Got me two Double Filet-O-Fishes. It was hard to take the bun off for health, but I stayed strong.

Nosey Lady started some canned food drive for Japan today. Idiot. They had an earthquake. It's not like they turned into Ethiopia. I told Nosey Lady if she wanted to send something to Japan, she should just send her prayers. Really shut her down. Who does Nosey think she's gonna send heavy canned food to? She doesn't know anyone in Japan. And the postage would be through the roof! I shipped a small box to Florida once, and it was like 30 bucks. Japan would at least be a hundred dollars. She's out of her mind. If anything, just send a check. Japanese people don't want our gross canned carrots. So insulting.

So far, Nosey Lady has collected tomato soup, that crappy can of carrots I bet she brought from home, and some Hormel Chili. Asked her if I could trade something for the Hormel. It's SO good. She said no. Stupid idiot. Japanese people probably hate chili. It'll just go to waste. And wasting food is a sin. And I could make a mean Coney dog with it. I like to jazz Hormel up with my own herbs and spices. That's the secret to Captain Karl's Coney Supremes.

I'm gettin' that Hormel Chili, damnit. I don't care what Nosey Lady says. Right is right. Plus, can't risk offending the Japanese people.

Gettin' outta work. Gotta go rush through supper with the fam so I can meet my bro Al for some cold ones. I got that Friday fever, you guys.

1:27 A.M.

Just got home. Left my lights on at the last bar me and Al went to. He already split. Had to call AAA to get a jump. Froze my keister off. Thought the AAA guy was gonna give me a hard time about bein' boozed up. He didn't care at all. Even bummed me a smoke. Jumped me and split. Think he mighta been on the sauce too. It was a guy code situation.

SATURDAY, MARCH 12, 2011-ATKINS DIET, DAY 69
(HA! JUST SOME GUY HUMOR.)

Cheat day is in full effect, you guys. Takin' Ann out for a nice supper tonight. Can't wait for Olive Garden. It's our special place.

SUNDAY, MARCH 13, 2011-ATKINS DIET, DAY 70

Me and Ann really had a feast at OG last night. Got pretty messed up too. Tried to give her my breadstick, if you catch my drift. Ha! Guess she was "feelin' too full" and had to hit the sack. Woke up on the couch this mornin' at Ann's to my daughters yelling, "Ew, Karl's on the couch in his tighties! Gross!" I threw on my Dockers and got the heck outta there. Shouldn't have to be that way. Don't think they understand I OWN THE FRIGGIN' HOUSE AND I DESERVE TO SLEEP IN COMFORT!

MONDAY, MARCH 14, 2011-ATKINS DIET, DAY 71

Nosey Lady asked me this morning, "What's wrong, Karl? You look sad." Idiot. It's Monday, I'm at work, you're talkin' to me, and I hate you. THAT'S what's wrong.

Brought in some canned corn to trade for the Hormel Chili in the food drive. Nosey Lady still said no. Sick of this. Might try to switch labels on the corn and chili. The cans are the same size. Gonna go do some recon on the donation box.

5:28 P.M.

Nosey Lady is about to go take her 5:30 crap break. I've been timing it every day and she's in the john way too long for #1. That's my window to pull the switch with the corn and chili. I think she takes craps right before goin' home to save on TP. She's so cheap. I just do it to waste time. That's the difference. I've got my glue and X-Acto knife ready. Feelin' really "covert ops" about the chili mission, you guys.

5:47 P.M.

Got the labels switched. Looks pretty good. Spilled some glue on my pants though. Looks like a gross "you know what" stain. Nosey Lady was so busy payin' attention to my fake "guy stain" that she didn't notice me put back the "chili." Sicko. Ha!

Off to Ann's for supper. Wait 'til everyone hears about how I totally scammed the Hormel from the Japanese donation box. It's pretty badass.

TUESDAY, MARCH 15, 2011—ATKINS DIET, DAY 72

Think Nosey Lady might be suspicious. She put a big sign on the donation box that says, "UNLESS YOUR DONATING, DON'T TOUCH." "Your"? Idiot.

Last night I tried to explain to my kids how I scored the chili so it wouldn't offend the Japanese people. They said it was "stealing." I told my kids that there's no such thing as "stealing" in politics. I think it was a good lesson. Sometimes kids need to learn the truth. Let 'em know that if anything, "stealing" that chili kinda makes me a quiet hero. They kinda look up to me, you guys. Plus, they won't think it's "stealing" when I make 'em up a batch of Captain Karl's Coney Supremes. Mm-mmmm!

Super pumped for St. Paddy's Day, you guys. Got my wearin' o' the green all picked out.

Picked up four 6-packs of Guinness for St. Paddy's pregamers. Couldn't resist though. Me and Dave went through half of 'em already. They go down so smooth. Nothin' wrong with celebratin' a little early anyway. It's cosmopolitan. Technically, St. Paddy's is a weeklong celebration in the big cities.

WEDNESDAY, MARCH 16, 2011–ATKINS DIET, DAY 73

Started feelin' "sick" at work at the end of the day so it won't be obvious when I take tomorrow off for St. Paddy's. It's a solid move.

Told Ann about Wing Wednesday so she make BAKED chicken wings for supper. They just aren't the same. Barely choked down a few to be polite, then stopped off for real ones after.

Super pumped for the big pub crawl tomorrow. Gonna hit Paddy's, Applebee's, Chili's, all the hot spots. Gotta do it right. Picked up a few more sixers of Guinness for tomorrow. Guess what? Me and Dave polished 'em off again. Happy St. Paddy's Eve, you guys! Might be too pumped to sleep. Gonna toss a Lunesta grenade in with the booze. Should do the trick, responsibly.

THURSDAY, MARCH 17, 2011–ATKINS DIET, DAY 74–ST. PADDY'S DAY
1:37 P.M.

Woke up kinda late. That Lunesta and booze combo conked me out. Dave already went and picked up some more Guinness. Used money from my wallet, but it's the thought that counts. Already cracked a few. Full steam ahead. Puttin' a corned beef in the Crock-Pot for sandwiches later. Gonna work up a mean hunger on the pub crawl.

2:34 P.M.

Just noticed I had two missed calls from work. Was so excited I forgot to call in sick. Had Dave blow in a jingle for me. He told Nosey Lady, "This is Karl's roommate. Karl is sick and can't get off the toilet." Great. Idiot. That's not the vibe I'm really tryin' to lay down at my place of employment. Screw it. I'll deal with Dave's crap story tomorrow. Nothin' can ruin St. Paddy's Day. Gonna pound one more Irish Car Bomb and I'm off to Applebee's.

2:47 P.M.

That last Car Bomb came back up on Dave. Had to get himself cleaned up. He's fine though. NOW it's time to get our Applebee's on!

10:32 P.M.

Just got home. Pretty messed up. Gotta lay down. Dave's passed out in the Sebring. Fine, stay there all night, I don't care.

FRIDAY, MARCH 18, 2011–ATKINS DIET, DAY 75

Just gettin' around. Took work off again. Told 'em I was dehydrated from my "stomach issues." Not really a lie at all. Had such a blast for St. Paddy's. Me, my bro Al, and Dave got pretty rowdy. Hit Chili's after Applebee's, where Dave puked a THIRD time. Dave was buyin' insane amounts of shots. He was super blotto. It was like we were in a George Thorogood song. Dave knocked over a whole freakin' table at the Chili's bar, then started playin' air guitar to music that wasn't even on! A few minutes later, he ran to the john. Then came out with no shirt on and his pants were all wet for whatever reason. It was time to GO. Me and Al had to drag Dave to the Sebring. He kept makin' crazy faces and screamin' embarrassing crap like "Free Bird!" for no reason. It was so great! I bet everyone at Chili's knows how we party now. Me, Al, and Dave must be kinda like the bad boys of Chili's bar.

Next we went to Paddy McGee's Irish Pub. You gotta close it out at an authentic Irish place, ya know? I got the Reuben Pizza. Always hits the spot. We had to leave Dave in the car. He passed out and wouldn't get up. Besides, good pals let you sleep it off 'til you're back in business. Me and Al were still rockin' though. Started takin' down $2.50, 24 oz. green beer drafts (told ya Paddy's was authentic). They even had Irish music on. Me and Al were crackin' jokes, laughin', just havin' a blast. Then Ann called to see when I'd be over for supper. Why would Ann think I'd have family supper on St. Paddy's Day?! It's a national tradition for guys to hit the pubs. Think she's kinda steamed.

After I told Ann, "We'll discuss this when it's not a holiday of celebration," me and Al got into what I like to call "The Welzein Zone." Shots, beers, shots, beers . . . man, we were goin' hard-core. Completely forgot about Dave in the cold car. He wandered in with no shirt and his wet pants, started to say somethin', then just puked on the floor. He got kicked out of Paddy's 30 seconds after walkin' in. It must be a new record or something. They shoulda gave him a gift certificate. Me and Al were just DYING, you guys.

I kinda blacked out after Dave barfed. Woke up this morning with the Crock-Pot still on. The corned beef was kinda dry but real tender. Dave was asleep in the bathtub this morning, covered in puke. He needs to learn some self-control. Musta wandered in after I blacked out and left him in the car.

Just noticed there's still some Guinness left over. Fake sick + Guinness lefties = chillin'.

8:45 P.M.

Had a few too many St. Paddy's Part 2 Guinnesses and crashed out. Forgot about supper with Ann and the kids. Again. I'm in Doghouse City. Ann doesn't understand that if there's brews to drink, you gotta drink 'em. It's guy code. Kinda like the samurais had in the Orient. I'm gonna try to kick back, you guys. Makin' a corned beef lefty sammie. I'm gonna make it up to the fam tomorrow. No biggie.

SATURDAY, MARCH 19, 2011—ATKINS DIET, DAY 76

Supposed to go to Ann and the kids' for early supper in a bit. I think she wants to have a "talk" about my behavior. Great. I don't see what the big deal is. I took off two little days from family time for St. Paddy's Day and all hell breaks loose. Lettin' loose for St. Paddy's is an American tradition. It's not like I had a choice. What if I told Ann not to get a Christmas tree?

Gonna try to smooth things over by gettin' us a pizza with all the toppings. Really go supreme. That should help. Pizza really brings families together.

Why can't wives just punch men in the plumbing instead of havin' "talks"? It's quicker and less painful.

SUNDAY, MARCH 20, 2011-ATKINS DIET, DAY 77

Feelin' kinda down. Had a pretty weak-end. I know I've had four days off, but still, bummed about facing the music tomorrow.

Thought the supreme pizzas would really wow Ann and the kids last night, but my son just used his magic wand to pick off all the toppings. I told him that "a real man likes his pizza with ALL the toppings." He said, "Why, Daddy?" Like I have time to answer that. And my daughters wouldn't even touch the supreme pizza. Said all they could taste were the "grody" green peppers. I really blew it with the supremes. After supper, Ann wanted to have that "talk." I just ate seven slices of supreme pizza. Do you want me to die of indigestion?

Ann said I wasn't really holding up to my bargain of "family supper time." I took two days off for a major drinking holiday! Jeez. Plus, when I come by, my daughters start in with the fatso jokes and then my son does some Tinker Bell magic crap. It's bad for my self-esteem. She doesn't understand that sometimes I need two or three days of "guy time" to let loose and drink a few cases of cold ones. I work hard. The whole time I just kept nodding my head in agreement, saying, "Yes, baby, I understand." Women only care if they're right, not if you listen. I don't feel all that bad lying to Ann about paying attention. It's ok for guys to lie when they don't get any action from their gal. Gotta go over to Ann and the kids' for supper AGAIN in a few. God, families just never end. At least I have a pretty solid scotch buzz goin'.

All this crap worked out for Dave though. I brought all those supreme pizza lefties home. He's in hog heaven. Keeps sayin' how it's like "Pizza Christmas." Dave LOVES toppings. It's one of the few things he actually does right.

MONDAY, MARCH 21, 2011–ATKINS DIET, DAY 78.

Had a 30-minute meeting with Nosey Lady this morning about "sick day policies." Does she really think people use sick days for when they're "sick"? Sick days are for goin' to Tigers games and boozin'. If I'm gonna spend the whole day in the can, I might as well get paid for it at work.

Oh, and guess who never shipped those canned goods? Nosey Lady. Maybe she should take care of Japan before worrying about MY life. If she doesn't ship those, they should be up for grabs. She just can't hog 'em all. So sick of Nosey Lady's crap.

Supper at Ann's tonight sucked. My son kept "flying" around on the Swiffer. That's not magic! At least learn a cool card trick or something. Plus, Ann's still giving me that "look" for what I "did." That was LAST week. I came to family dinner TONIGHT. Get over it. And she made some weird curry hippie crap. Stopped off for a Burger King Triple Stacker on the way home (no bun). Healthy food doesn't have to taste like BO.

Today sucked. Everything sucks. Everyone sucks. Sick of this. I'm gonna drink some friggin' cold ones and forget this stupid weather and my stupid life.

TUESDAY, MARCH 22, 2011-ATKINS DIET, DAY 79.

We were talkin' about what celebrities people looked like at work today. Nosey Lady said I looked like "a husky Barry Gibb." Got so steamed.

Hmm, let's see what's on the docket for tonight?! Oh. Great! Supper with Ann and the kids! Can't wait. Why do I even bother waking up and breathing in the morning?

SATURDAY, MARCH 26, 2011-ATKINS DIET, DAY 83

Real doozy last night. Guess I was a little overserved before I met the fam at Big Boy for supper. Cold ones were goin' down so smooth. Can't really blame me. I had a rough week at work. A man's gotta unwind somehow, you guys. And for me, that somehow is with $2.50, 24 oz. drafts. I musta had five or six before I met them out. Was in no mood for their boring crap. My kids are a snoozefest. They gave me guff for gettin' waffle fries on the side with my Super Big Boy hamburg. They don't know anything about responsible eating after a few beverages. Plus, I was paying for those burgers.

One of my daughters said I was turning into the "Big Boy." I got so steamed I knocked over my son's milkshake and he started BAWLING. I told him to put a lid on it and try to fix his shake with "magic." He actually tried. It was pathetic so I just got him another one. Told him money is real, not magic. It was a quality lesson.

Ann was a little burned up that I was on the sauce. It was FRI-DAY. We have to compromise. I came to dinner, for Pete's sake. Might have to talk with Ann about not havin' family dinner on Friday and Saturday. Everyone should have a break from their family. It's healthy. Told her I couldn't make it to supper tonight. "Comin' down with a head cold." Me and Dave ordered a supreme pie. Sippin' whiskey. That's good for colds. I figure if you're doin' things that you do when you're sick, what's the difference if you're actually sick or not? Same diff. And for me, when I'm sick, I like a nice supreme pizza and some whiskey. Always does the trick. And Cheetos. Cheetos are good too. Why don't places offer Crunchy Cheetos as a pizza topping? Seems like a no-brainer. Captain Karl's Pizza Ship should definitely have Cheetos Pizza. Gotta write that down. I should tell Papa John about my Cheetos topping idea instead of Domino's. Papa John seems like a cool guy. "Papa's in the house!" And he hooks it up with garlic butter dippin' sauce. Wish they sold that in a bottle at the supermarket. I'd put it on everything. Papa John kinda reminds me of myself. Just a laid-back dude with a cool car who likes good grub. Guy Fieri on Triple D too. Been thinkin' about tryin' out a new look. Maybe get a cut like Guy's? Maybe just ONE earring though. Don't wanna be a copycat.

SUNDAY, MARCH 27, 2011–ATKINS DIET, DAY 84

Told Ann I'd only come over for supper if we could watch the Pistons while we eat. She said ok. Damnit, thought that'd get me out of it. I'm bringin' a 12-pack too. If I leave it here, Dave'll hog it all down. Can't watch the Pistons without cold ones.

I wish my son would watch b-ball with me. Tried to get him into it once and he just kept sayin' how it wasn't as good as some made-up "Quidditch" crap from those stupid movies he likes. I told him you just can't make up sports. They either exist or they don't. Michael Jordan didn't just invent some fake crap to be good at. My son needs to learn that pretend things like imagination and magic are just gonna get him a smack in the face from the real world, and ZERO babes.

MONDAY, MARCH 28, 2011-ATKINS DIET, DAY 85

Just can't handle work today. Spent most of the day seriously considering having a severe stapler accident just so I could leave.

Well, off to Ann and the kids' for supper! Should be a blast! Sometimes my whole life feels like punishment for something I didn't do.

TUESDAY, MARCH 29, 2011-ATKINS DIET, DAY 86

Was kinda slackin' on my diet, but I'm back in the saddle. Got five of the new shrimp tacos from Taco Bell. No shell. Pretty gourmet for Taco Bell. The shrimp were marinated just right, and the Creamy Avocado Ranch really knocked my socks off. Plus, it was super healthy. Red Lobster better look out, looks like Taco Bell might be makin' a move to be the king of seafood. And such a great value too.

I told Ken at work all about the shrimp tacs. He said he gets better ones when he visits Cali. "Cali"? Whoa, look at Mr. World Traveler over here.

Headin' to Ann and the kids' for supper. Unless I get lucky and don't make it 'cause I swerved into oncoming traffic or a building or something.

WEDNESDAY, MARCH 30, 2011-ATKINS DIET, DAY 87

If it weren't for Wing Wednesday, don't think I'd have a reason to even get up or be alive today. Focusing on the important things in life helps you be more positive. Doesn't change the fact that I have to go to family supper later though.

THURSDAY, MARCH 31, 2011-ATKINS DIET, DAY 88

Last night my son was crying 'cause my daughters kept calling him "gaytarded." I told him not to act that way if he doesn't like it 'cause kids can be cruel. I mean, I've got nothin' against gay people or retardeds. But when you act like both at the same time, you're gonna get called out. If he wants to be gaytarded, I'm open-minded and cool with it. It's 2011. But he can't get mad about bein' called that, especially when no one knows exactly what it means.

Goin' to supper with Ann and the kids. Might hit Paddy's after. It is Thirstday, after all.

11:56 P.M.

Just back from Paddy's. $3.50 wine special. Lotta gals. Real smokin' babes. Just hot babes everywhere, you guys. I told Dave he's gotta start hittin' up Paddy's for wine night. I've got the whole wife thing goin' on, so I can't go all the way, but I'm a great wingman. I got moves. Tonight, I musta bought these two gals a dozen glasses of wine. Man, they were hammered. Again, too bad I've got the Ann thing goin' on, I coulda really cut loose. Man, I am bombed. I ever tell you guys how Ann had the second biggest boobs in high school? That's how good my moves are. Real smooth.

Dave was tryin' to crash out, but he said he'll stay up and hang if I spring for the WrestleMania pay-per-view on Sunday. Whatever. Can't be more than $5.99.

FRIDAY, APRIL 1, 2011–ATKINS DIET, DAY 89

Dave had a stroke last night. Crapped himself and everything. Spent all night in the hospital. Made me lose so much sleep. Really draggin' today. And his crap smell is really reekin' up the Sebring. So steamed.

April Fools', you guys! Dave didn't really have a stroke. He's still the same old sack of garbage. Ann still thinks he did though. Ha! Might have to take advantage for some free time.

Was sippin' some Bloody Karls with Dave, tryin' to have a Saturday. Ann called and wanted to know if I would join her and the kids for 5:00 mass. Sure, right after I slam my nuts with this claw hammer. If Catholics REALLY wanted to be like Jesus, they'd spend an hour at a soup kitchen every week instead of church. I wouldn't do that either, but still. It's the thought. And just because I don't go to church doesn't mean I'm not Catholic. I grew up Catholic. I was an altar boy too. And no priest hanky-panky, I'd like to add. I'm ALL man. But that meant going to extra funerals to serve and crap, so I've put in plenty of time for the Big Man. Even got married to Ann in a Catholic Church out of respect to my babe. Thing is, nowadays, mass just doesn't rock, especially on the weekend. There's too much good sports, and TV quality has really come a long way. Maybe if they had cold ones after church for the ADULTS instead of coffee and donuts, I might consider it. But church doesn't even try to meet me halfway, so why should I make an effort with worship and crap?

Besides, me and Dave made plans to hit Arby's. Dave kinda blew my mind today. Told me that if you close your eyes, Arby's tastes like thin-sliced big brown hot dogs. My world is kinda flipped upside down right now. Need some time to think.

3:38 A.M.

Can't sleep. Been thinkin' 'bout me and Ann's wedding. Everything was so simple then. I looked badass in my tux, and Ann was so foxy in her dress. Her cans looked dynamite. There weren't any kids in the way, it was just me and her against the world. Even remember my vows:

I, Karl, take thee, Ann, to be my wife . . . all that other crap, etc. Then added on my own special sentiment: *You're pretty much the #1 woman for me, and that's why when I say we'll be together forever, you know I'm gonna keep on truckin'.*

Man, that was such a cool line. You don't just say somethin' like that unless you mean it.

SUNDAY, APRIL 3, 2011–ATKINS DIET, DAY 91

Me and Dave are super hungover. Got pretty bombed after Arby's. It's a great base to dump booze on. Could really go for some Mickey D's right now. Heard they deliver if you're handicapped. Dave kinda is, so it's worth a shot. If not, might just nurse a few domestics. Liquid breakfast never hurt anybody.

MONDAY, APRIL 4, 2011–ATKINS DIET, DAY 92

Was super hungover this morning, you guys. Hit a parked car on the way to work while I was jammin' full blast to "Beat It." Didn't see any damage while I drove away, so that was cool. As long as you don't see any damage, it's legal to just take off.

Not a lot of smoothness goin' on today. Went directly in the john to take a nap on the toilet and some grossout had whizzed all over the seat. Now my Dockers are all pee-stained. Then Dave called all freakin' out 'cause we forgot to watch WrestleMania yesterday. Apparently I'm paying for it. Forgot I even agreed to that. Dave said I ordered it drunk the other night. It was 60 bucks! Super P.O.'d, you guys. Just wanna kill Dave.

These pee pants are really grossing me out. It's all dried now, but I still know the pee is there. Dried pee is still pee. I told Ann I'd be late for supper 'cause I had to change my pee pants. She started laughing and dropped the phone. I didn't get to explain! There's a TON of ways to get pee on your pants. Not just peeing your pants.

Most people have had some kind of pee encounter. It's just part of life to get other people's pee on you sometimes.

TUESDAY, APRIL 5, 2011-ATKINS DIET, DAY 93

Why does Tuesday even exist? What a stupid excuse for a day.

Supper yesterday was a nightmare. Ann told the kids about my pee pants issue, so the kept calling me "Captain Pee Pants." Got really steamed. My son still uses damn plastic sheets on his bed. He's got no right to point his finger at me for havin' a pee pants incident. I told him, "When you wet the bed more often than you don't, you should keep your trap shut about other people's pee pants issues." Then he started in with the crybaby stuff. Sometimes you have to really break your kid down to teach him a lesson. Really destroy him.

Ann finally asked, "Well, what was the best part of your day?" The best part of my day is just about the same every day. After I leave stupid family supper and get about four beers in.

Ann's been hinting that I shoulda moved back in by now. I mean, if she wants to have a real conversation about it, I'm down. But I can't be expected to make all the effort. Sometimes the guy in the relationship likes to feel special too. "Hinting" just doesn't cut it.

WEDNESDAY, APRIL 6, 2011-ATKINS DIET, DAY 94

Don't know why I try at anything sometimes.

SATURDAY, APRIL 9, 2011

Gonna smoke some weed. I'm sick of everything. That's when it's time to smoke some weed. Kids shouldn't smoke weed. Or drug addicts. But if you're an adult, smokin' weed is ok if you have a job, you guys.

Had to get my Dell cleaned and fixed. Dave smoked too much weed and spilled Papa John's garlic sauce in the keyboard. He got all freaked out 'cause it was the last dippin' sauce and started MASH-ING pizza on my keyboard. Idiot. Took it to the "Geek Squad." More like "Barely-Got-a-GED Squad." Acted like they never saw a garlic dippin' sauce incident before. There's no way I'm the first person to mess up their laptop with Papa John's dippin' sauce. They acted like I was stupid. Told Dave he owes me 75 bucks. He said Papa John's should pay for it. Really steamed, you guys.

Dave kinda has a point. Papa John's garlic butter dippin' sauce must cause lots of disasters. Maybe they SHOULD be held respon-sible? Have to swing by and ask the manager.

The key to a good Wing Wednesday is to get two dozen so you have lefties for a healthy afternoon snack. I love 'em room temp. Brings out the flavor. Everyone knows that room temp pizza is the best. The fridge makes it all stale and kills the flavor. And I like BIG flavor. KFC is also best at room temp.

Headed to Ann's for supper. Still full of wings. Just gonna tell her I'm still on a diet so I don't have to eat any of her crud. She just doesn't understand that I like bold flavors just like Guy Fieri. Tuna casserole isn't very money, you guys. Might try and give her a hand in the kitchen tonight. Really show her how I drive the bus to Flavor Town.

Really lookin' forward to the weekend, you guys.

Tried to take Ann to Flavor Town last night. The tuna casserole was off the hook when I added my secret herbs and spices. The kids wouldn't touch the tuna casserole after I kicked it up. Way too out of bounds for them. They just don't like bold flavors, I guess. My son started gagging and saying his throat burned. That's what bold flavors do sometimes! I bet Guy Fieri's son Hunter isn't like that. I brought all the lefties home for Dave since no one could eat it. He destroyed 'em. Dave loves goin' to Flavor Town for Captain Karl's Money Tuna Cass.

SUNDAY, APRIL 17, 2011

Got into a pretty heavy discussion with Dave last night. We both agree, Bobby Flay kinda needs a good old-fashioned ass-kicking. Seems too big for his britches. I bet he shakes in his shoes when a real man like Guy Fieri comes around. Guy would clean his clock.

MONDAY, APRIL 18, 2011

Really draggin' today, you guys. Gotta start gettin' my body tight for summer. It's just so hard to think about gettin' that summertime beach body when it's so rainy and crappy all the time.

Ken walked in the john when I was doin' some push-ups. I stood up fast and cracked my head on the sink. Got a huge goose egg. Ken started laughin' his butt off. I'd like to see that wimp try to do nine 'shups in the middle of the day. The Japanese do exercises at work. I saw it in *Gung Ho*. Great flick. Teaches you a lot about cultural relations. Ken's an idiot.

TUESDAY, APRIL 19, 2011

Another crappy day. Sometimes I don't think I'll be able to get my boat out or play golf ever again. Makes me wanna kill myself.

Supper last night was awful. Ann made some diet food she

learned from Oprah. Why would you go on a diet that makes you a fat black gal? I can see if Halle Berry had a diet. She's smokin'. The only diet worth a crap is Atkins. It lets you have bold flavors and all the taste of your favorite foods like meats and cheeses.

FRIDAY, APRIL 22, 2011

Whatchu talkin' 'bout, Friday?! Ha! Man, gonna get bombed tonight like never before. Been thinkin' 'bout havin' a talk with Ann. Gotta man up. Don't know if things are workin' out for me. We might have different goals in life. She's just not a go-getter like myself.

8

GOTTA TAKE ADVANTAGE

APRIL 26–JUNE 11, 2011

TUESDAY, APRIL 26, 2011

Had to go on a stupid Easter egg hunt with my son on Saturday, hungover. Stepped on a plastic egg in my Tevas and rolled my ankle bad. Been laid up with my bum foot at Ann's. "Think I tore a ligament." I'm really milking it for all it's worth, gettin' the full service. I told my son it was his fault I had to go to the stupid egg hunt. Made him bring me cold ones and ham all weekend like a slave!

Showed up four hours late for work today on crutches. No one cared that I was late! I must say, being crippled is pretty great, you guys. Ken asked how I hurt my ankle. Told him I kicked in a door, bad boy style. Don't wanna take any guff for "I stepped on an Easter egg." Kickin' in a door is the most badass way to hurt your ankle. Probably happened to guys like T.J. Hooker and Hunter all the time. Just told work, "Oh brother, my ankle hurts so bad. Sorry, gotta go home and ice it." More like, "Ice my throat with a cold one." Ha!

Headed to Ann's for supper. Told her I need a nice, fat, juicy steak pronto when I get there. She said ok! This is the life, you guys.

WEDNESDAY, APRIL 27, 2011

Hope this sprained ankle lasts as long as possible. Crippled people really are livin' the dream. Freebies and sympathy are where it's at. My son feels so bad about my sprain. "I hurt Daddy!" What a crybaby. Still, nice to know he respects his hero.

Nosey Lady asked if I have a doctor's note 'cause I was late for work. I'm on crutches! Doctor's notes are for when you FAKE being sick. Idiot. Headin' to Ann's early for supper. Told Nosey I have a doctor's appointment. If she wants to tangle with me, let's get it on! Ann's makin' me some feel-better pork chops. Wives are really great when you need them for something. Those chops better have bold flavors though.

FRIDAY, APRIL 29, 2011

Get outta my dreams, get into my Friday! Really lookin' forward to the weekend, you guys. It's almost 60 degrees outside. I'd almost think about gettin' the boat out if it weren't for my bum ankle. Sure do miss my baby.

Nosey Lady thinks I should be healed up by now and still wants to see a doctor's note for my tardiness. I'm not a 4th grader. Idiot. I know when my bod is 110%.

11:45 P.M.

Hit Paddy's for a few cold ones with Al and Dave. Gina was such a sweetheart. Even signed my Ace bandage and gave me a little cheek smooch. Cripples must get all the babes.

Makin' me and Dave a Tombstone pizza a la Captain Karl. Really jazzin' it up with my own herbs and spices. Flavor is gonna be outta bounds. I bet when Guy Fieri makes a Tombstone, that bad boy is the mayor of Flavor Town. He's probably the best chef in the USA right now.

SATURDAY, APRIL 30, 2011

Just woke up on the couch. Passed out before I could get after that Tombstone. Looks like Dave hogged it all down. Really steamed. When one man makes another man a supreme pizza, you at least leave him a few slices for the effort. It's guy code.

SUNDAY, MAY 1, 2011

Yesterday took a bad turn when Dave tried to do a karate spin kick and fell on my bum ankle. He broke a lamp though, which was pretty cool. Also, I bet him $5 he couldn't do two spin kicks in a row, so I scored a fiver.

My ankle kills since Dave fell on it. My bro Al gave me some Vicodin. Popped a couple with a few brewskis to wash 'em down. I'm all fuzzy. I feel fuzzy. Like a fuzzy, fuzzy Muppet.

Why do I wear shirts all the time? Don't need this shirt. Feels good to have it off. Gonna not wear a shirt and drink another cold one, you guys.

MONDAY, MAY 2, 2011

Slept in. Forgot it was Monday. Just got the good word about Bin Laden though. See, that's why you don't mess with the USA, you guys. Looks like I picked the right day to miss work. There's no way anyone went in. It's gotta be the biggest party of the year. Sent Dave to the store for some Budweisers and Johnsonvilles. Beautiful day out. Gonna fire up the grill for the red, white, and blue! What a great Monday. We should kill a terrorist every week. Just a real treat.

No, Ann. I don't want to be picked up for supper. When I tell you "my ankle's too sore to drive over," it means "I'm drinkin' and I need to be left alone."

TUESDAY, MAY 3, 2011

Got some looks at work like, "Still on crutches, huh?" It actually hurts really bad now! Don't think anyone buys the Dave spin kick story. I forget how boring some people's lives are that it's inconceivable to them that I bet my roomie $5 he couldn't do two spin kicks in a row. Me and Dave are probably two of the hardest partiers in the Flint area. Work people just look at me as the guy who clogged the toilet once. I bet if Nosey Lady could see my night moves, it'd blow her mind. Maybe I'd get more respect or sympathy sometimes.

WEDNESDAY, MAY 4, 2011

Ate a big batch of my off-the-chain Sloppy UnJoes before bed 'cause Ann's chicken and rice supper didn't have the bold flavors I crave. Guess I added too many hot peppers to the dish 'cause my backdoor was in flames all night.

Woke up in the john this mornin' to stupid Dave takin' a shower. Me and Dave should never, EVER be in the same room while he's in the nude. Dave is a psychopath sometimes. Why the hell would you do that? Just wake me up. I don't know if I'll ever get over this. To be clear, I didn't actually see Dave's peener and veggies, but the idea that they were in the same room with me is puke city. I played football and stuff in high school, but I was never one to hang out in the shower and play grab-ass after the game. Not my style.

THURSDAY, MAY 5, 2011

Work didn't do ANYTHING for the Cinco. So disrespectful to the Mexican people on their biggest day of the year, you guys.

So excited to whip up a batch of my world-famous Captain Karl's Special Recipe Margs I can hardly sit still. I make THE best margs. Got some Taco Bell for el luncho, but only had five Grilled Steak Soft Tacs. Kept it simple for that authentic Mexican taste in honor of the celebration. Always admired the Mexican people. They love bold flavors, cold ones, and takin' it easy. If I was Mexican, I'd party like Cinco de Mayo every day.

Ann just called to say she's makin' Taco Salad for supper. No es muy bueno. Got no time for that, I gotta get home to make my margs! Plus, Taco Salad doesn't have the authentic bold flavors I crave. Ann uses "French" dressing. So stupid. Plus, Mexicans didn't invent Taco Salad 'til like 1983. Told Ann, "Sorry, babe. Can't come by tonight. Dave planned a big fiesta and I can't let down my main man." Yeah right he did. Ha! Dave did say he wants to head out later 'cause "the saucy Latinos will all be horned up." Hope he meant "Latinas." I worry about him sometimes.

SUNDAY, MAY 8, 2011

Me and Dave are takin' out a KFC bucket. Got the chicken grilled to keep it healthy, but Dave is straight up drinkin' gravy, so it's a wash. Still, we're keepin' it chillin'. Gotta love a do-nothin' Sunday, you guys.

Crap. Just realized it's Mother's Day. Gonna finish up this 12-pack and watch the end of the hoops game. Probably hit 7-Eleven for some gifts.

MONDAY, MAY 9, 2011

Really went all out for Mom's Day. Got Ann a chocolate rose, giant novelty card, and a copy of *Date Night* from 7-Eleven. Sometimes simple, thoughtful gifts are the best. No need for fancy Zales jewelry and all that crap. 7-Eleven does Mom's Day just fine, you guys.

And, 'cause I didn't show up to Ann's 'til 10 o'clock last night, without a phone call or anything, she thought it was a huge surprise. Ann wouldn't hardly talk to me. I think she was kinda choked up from my thoughtfulness. Captain Karl knows how to treat the ladies. Plus, when you go to 7-Eleven for Mom's Day gifts, you can get yourself a Chili Cheese Big Bite as a reward. They're such a classic. Headin' over to Ann's now for supper. I bet she's still ridin' high. Tip: 7-Eleven, never forget, for great gifts.

TUESDAY, MAY 10, 2011

Guess I stand corrected on my Mom's Day gifts from the Sev. Musta been a little buzzed when I forked 'em over. Ann's pretty steamed. She keeps doing that fake crazy smile and sayin', "Oh, everything's fine, Karl." Oh, SO sorry I didn't go to Zales. Whatever happened to "It's the thought that counts"? Last night she showed me her home-made Mom's Day cards from the kids like they were so special. Homemade cards just say you were too thoughtless to go to the store.

Thinkin' 'bout really wowing Ann with a gift "that I ordered but it arrived late." Make her feel terrible about how generous I am. Might give her this necklace from Zales so she shuts up about Mom's Day. She loves that *Cougar Town* show.

WEDNESDAY, MAY 11, 2011

Gave Ann the cougar necklace tonight. She thought it was a joke. Really hurt my feelings. Drinkin' 'em away. Far, far, away.

THURSDAY, MAY 12, 2011

Really draggin'. Too many cold ones last night. Might be a toilet nap kinda day.

Got some good news today. My bro Al wants to go to the Tigers game on Saturday. Look out, Comerica, the Welzein bad boys are comin'! Super pumped, you guys. Can't wait, can't wait, can't wait! Man, drinkin' some roadies on the way down to Comerica, maybe have a few stogies. Might be just what I needed. It's ok to drink while you're driving to a sporting event or a concert. But only if you're an adult with a cool car or a conversion van. And especially if you're rockin' some Allman Bros.

FRIDAY, MAY 13, 2011

Stupid work kept us there late. Means I got a late start on boozin'. Gotta soak up some of the drinks with this turkey-and-American on a burrito shell with hot sauce. It's a new twist on an old classic. And healthy so I can really indulge at the Tigs game tomorrow. Screw it, gonna make a few more.

SUNDAY, MAY 15, 2011

Really had a blast with Al at the game yesterday. Daiquiris were in full order. Went down SO smooth. Musta had eight of 'em by the 5th inning. I usually don't like to overdo it, but it's kind of a tradition to get really bombed at a baseball game. Plus, it amps up the excitement. Me and Al sat behind some loudmouth Royals fans. Al told 'em to "suck my ass" about a thousand times. Al'd be great at a Friars roast. When they turned around, I told 'em, "You don't want a piece of the Welzein bad boys." Me and Al high-fived and did a quick pose-down. They totally left. Ha! It was definitely a high point. But man, when I got a "Let's go Tigers!" chant goin' on in the john? Felt on top of the world.

We were really rockin' it when Al bet me $5 I couldn't eat six hot dogs. Cost me almost $40, but I had to get it on. A bet's a bet. Really took 'em down. Didn't know my own strength! After that, we were asked to leave the game for some reason I don't remember, so we hit Cheli's Chili. It's just the best for afties. Cheli's might be the best sports bar in the country. Their homemade chili is out of bounds with bold flavor, and their 14 Hour Smoke Pulled Pork and Brisket are so tender you could eat it all day with an ice cream scoop. Me and Al started off with Fried Canadian Rib Tips. Really off the chain. Then we went for the Cheli's Chili Nachos. Just dynamite. But what really took me to Flavor Town was the Cheli's Chili 4-Way. Chili and fixins OVER spaghetti. So money, you guys. Guy Fieri would go bananas. We took down about eight more Labatts, and that's when Al broke the toilet and we had to leave. Cheli's Chili Bar is just the best.

MONDAY, MAY 16, 2011

Gettin' back on a health kick. Ate JUST the insides of three Taco Bell Beefy Melt Burritos. Just snip off the tops and enjoy with a fork.

I call 'em Beefy Melt Travelers. Taco Bell should sell 'em that way for folks lookin' to get that beach bod on point.

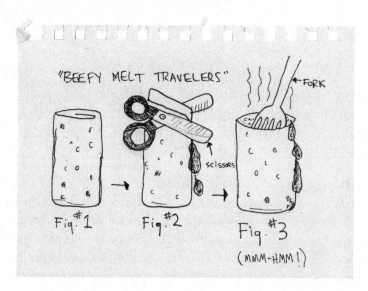

Gonna force out a healthy BM before I head to Ann and the kids' for supper. Really grunt out the sucker. Don't wanna have to take any crap about my bathroom issues 'cause of my diet.

TUESDAY, MAY 17, 2011

Last night, the kids were askin' why I had to have supper on the couch. Ann told 'em it's because I "pooped my back out." Which was true (grunted too hard) but really unnecessary. It started an hour-long conversation about "how" and "why" I pooped my back out. Made me feel like an idiot. Gonna have a few cold ones to relax. Supper was crap. Work was crap. Wife is crap. Kids are crap. Everything's crap but these cold ones.

WEDNESDAY, MAY 18, 2011

Feelin' kinda down. Think I'm just burned out on not havin' any romantic satisfaction. Relationships are tough. But when you find a special gal, you gotta just drag it out even if neither of you are happy. That's what love is.

THURSDAY, MAY 19, 2011

Really lookin' forward to the weekend, you guys.

Got six pieces of Kentucky GRILLED chicken for lunch today. Gonna look SO good this summer. Can't wait for Ann to see me in my trunks.

FRIDAY, MAY 20, 2011

Really bummed. Macho Man Randy Savage died. Treated myself to the Sizzling Smokehouse Chicken Stack and a few Sam Adams for lunch at Applebee's. Isn't sittin' well. Guess I'm too sad for digestion. I mean, unless they screwed it up. The Sizzling Smokehouse Chicken Stack is chicken breast seasoned with BBQ spices, then topped with shaved ham, applewood smoked bacon, and melted cheddar cheese. Served on two corn cakes with a BBQ demi-glace and a side of cheesy corn. Seems like a no-brainer. Nosey Lady asked why I looked down. Told her about Randy. She said, "Oh c'mon, the Slim Jim guy?" Then walked away. Made me so steamed. I'm leaving. Gonna have a proper weekend for the Macho Man. A TRUE American hero.

SATURDAY, MAY 21, 2011

Really hurtin'. Went all out for Randy last night. My cell phone is all smashed to pieces. Jumped off the couch to do a Macho elbow drop on Dave. Had it in my pocket. Huge bruise on my thigh. Looks kinda badass though. Wish beach season was here so I could show it off, you guys.

SUNDAY, MAY 22, 2011

Was watchin' *True Lies*. Jamie Lee Curtis was lookin' SMOKIN' hot. Dave said she has a peener and it was gay to like her. Idiot. Sweet cans make up for a lady peener you won't see anyway.

Man, I sure am drunk, you guys. Sometimes accidents happen for no reason on Sundays. Cold ones go down SO smooth when it's crappy outside and you're arguin' about Jamie Lee Curtis's sweet, sweet cans.

THURSDAY, MAY 26, 2011

Bad news for Memorial Day weekend. Weather report says it's gonna be pourin' down cold ones, brats, and good times. Ha!

Memorial Day weekend is the time we drink up all the booze and eat up all the grub that the soldiers didn't get to. It's important. If I went out on the battlefield in a blaze of glory or even a helicopter crash, I'd damn sure want everyone partyin' hard for Captain Karl.

Pickin' up this bad boy for the celebration:

Can't believe we have to work tomorrow. The troops deserve AT LEAST a four-day weekend. Three days isn't nearly enough partyin' for their sacrifice. Might fake sick tomorrow and stay home. Lying isn't wrong if you're doin' it to support the USA, you guys.

FRIDAY, MAY 27, 2011

Did the right thing, didn't fake the runs, and went into work 'cause they gave us a half-day. Never waste a lie you can use later. I can burn up a half-day with real runs in the john, no problem.

SATURDAY, MAY 28, 2011

Really blew it yesterday. Was so pumped I think I made several batches of my special margs too strong. Either that or it was an old batch of tequila that was past the freshness date. Never be sure. Looks like I smashed the bottle in the bathtub.

Ann wants me to come over for a BBQ tomorrow. Jeez. Memorial Day weekend is about cold ones and America, not families like at Christmas. I better take advantage of my freedom I have today that people sacrificed for.

SUNDAY, MAY 29, 2011

Headin' to the BBQ. Four hours late. Ann's britches are all in a twist about it. I needed a nap. Slept in the 'Bring last night. I shouldn't be in trouble 'cause I was responsible and crashed out in my car after Paddy's last night. Blackin' out and drivin' don't mix, you guys.

Four hours late or not, there better be some good grub left. Bringin' my own seasonings. The only thing Ann kicks up in the kitchen are bland flavors.

Got pretty messed up at Ann's yesterday. Went pretty heavy on the margs and she was all out of the eats. Ate potato salad on a hot dog bun. A potato salad dog isn't actually too bad when I kick it up with some spicy mustard and my secret seasoning blend.

Got into it pretty bad with Tina Carlson. She called me "Big Karl." Got steamed and muttered that she was a "big gross bitch." When I'm bombed on margs, you do NOT want to get in the ring with me, especially if you look like Tina Carlson. I know some great insults and put-downs. And for the record, I'd never call a woman the B-word if I wasn't provoked and/or drunk on a holiday. You gotta respect the ladies, you guys.

Guess I took my shirt off to show Tina my beach bod. She started laughing. I may have a stomach, but it's firm. Not like Tina's sloppers. Her husband Doug, who's a real load, got all P.O.'d that I was burning Tina, so I challenged him to a pose-down, like a real man. Doug wouldn't even take his shirt off. Just walked away like a wuss. He really embarrassed himself. I was pretty exhausted from all the confrontation and margs. Fell asleep on the deck with no shirt on in a lawn chair. Ann locked me outside and went to bed, I guess. So rude. Why'd you even invite me over?!

Gonna patch it up and do it RIGHT for the troops today. Brats, ribs, all the trimmings, Cool Ranch D'reets. Full spread. The works, really. And of course, plenty of Rum-and-Hawaiian-Punch. It's Dave's specialty for the holiday. Goin' down so smooth. Fruit juice gets you hydrated as well as gives the body nutrients.

TUESDAY, MAY 31, 2011

Really draggin' today. They should really give us a day off for some R&R after a long weekend like that. No one's gonna do any work anyway. Only good thing about today are all the brat lefties I packed for lunch. Brought six of 'em. No bun. Tryin' to get back on my diet program.

Think Ann's still steamed about Sunday's incidents, callin' Tina's breasts "sloppers," etc. She said not to come for supper. Guess I just have to eat whatever I want while I watch the Tigers game. Boo-hoo. Thanks for the punishment. Like it's wrong to pass out in a lawn chair on a major holiday. If anything, it's a RIGHT, for hardworkin' fellas all across the USA.

WEDNESDAY, JUNE 1, 2011

Just took down 18 Mango Habaneros for Wing Wednesday. Really packed a punch. Off the hook with bold flavors. Sweat through my shirt and had to change. The only thing I had in the car was an Under Armour muscle tee for my workouts. I'm sure it was a treat for the gals at work. My arms were lookin' buff, but no one likes a show-off. Decided to go home and change. Got sucked into a few *Dog the Bounty Hunter*s at the pad. Such a nice break. Should take one every day. Feel like I'd be a good bounty hunter. One thing I firmly believe in is street justice. Plus, you get to wear fingerless gloves like a real bad boy.

Went back to work and then headed to Ann and the kids' for supper. There wasn't anyone home and she won't answer her phone. Kinda worried. No way she's still steamed about Sunday. I mean, it's great to have a bachelor's supper. I just hope nothin's wrong. This isn't like Ann to disappear without tellin' me. Thinkin' good thoughts. Gonna have a few Crown-and-Diets to take the edge off.

11:45 P.M.

Ann never called. Kinda late, but gonna call Ann. Almost outta Crown. Really wanna make sure she's safe before I hit the sack.

12:07 A.M.

Ann didn't pick up. Callin' Ann back.

12:50 A.M.

Gonna try Ann again. Gotta catch some z's.

1:32 A.M.

Keeps goin' straight to voicemail. Time to hit the sack. Outta Crown anyway. Hope she's ok.

THURSDAY, JUNE 2, 2011

Ann just called. Said she didn't appreciate all the late-night phone calls. I was worried. Of course I got a little drunk. Guess she took the kids out for Chinese. Coulda told me. Feel left out. She's still sore from the Memorial Day thing. Families can be cruel sometimes. Ann knows I love the bold flavors of the Orient. We never get to go out for supper when I come over and have to choke down her garbage. Maybe I just care too much?

FRIDAY, JUNE 3, 2011

Had a nice, healthy homemade salad for lunch. Diced up four Jr. Bacon Cheeseburgers from Wendy's. (No buns. Special diet recipe.) Wendy's should really put the Jr. Bacon Cheeseburger Salad on their menu. "Where's the beef? It's in the salad, you stupid old bag." Ha!

Gonna hit Wild Spurs next to Paddy's late night for karaoke. Might do some numbers. Show the Wild Spurs country babes my pipes. Goin' heavy on the Axe Spiked-Up Look hair gel. Kinda got a Guy Fieri look goin'. Feelin' good! Look out, gals, Captain Karl's on the prowl.

SATURDAY, JUNE 4, 2011

Karaoke was really slammin' last night at Wild Spurs. Did "Livin' on a Prayer." EVERYONE sang along. Felt on top of the world! When you have a gift like singing, sometimes it doesn't really shine through 'til you've had eight or so cocktails. I think I might have the chops. People were buyin' me drinks after I did Bon Jovi. Kinda know how he must feel after a show. The rock 'n' roll lifestyle really has its perks. Man, and the crowd just went bonkers after I took my shirt off for the last verse. My diet must be really payin' off. I really shoulda joined a band when I was younger. Coulda been a huge star. Havin' a family really crushes all the dreams you didn't know you had.

Might do Van Halen's "Jump" next week. If they liked Bon Jovi, they'll lose their crap for Diamond Dave. Not-Diamond "Dave" said we should do a duet next week. When you're a rocker, everyone wants a piece of your spotlight. Told him no. I'm not tryin' to send out the wrong message like Hall & Oates, if you know what I mean.

Think I'm gonna head over to Wild Spurs. Maybe see some of my new karaoke pals from last night. They really get the rock 'n' roll lifestyle like I do.

SUNDAY, JUNE 5, 2011

Just found an old copy of *Penthouse* under the sink. I'm a *Penthouse* man from way back, you guys. Dave's been givin' me crap for it. Idiot. Jack mags aren't just for jackin'. They can be for readin' too. I'm not some animal. As a *Penthouse* man, sometimes enjoyin' the foxy babes for their beauty is enough. You don't always have to work on your plumbing, you guys. I told Dave, when there's a racy scene with a dynamite gal like Demi Moore, I just don't start tuggin' away in the theater. Gotta have some class. Masturbation is a personal private thing for your shower, your own room, or your car. Keep it to yourself. No one wants to know your business.

MONDAY, JUNE 6, 2011

Brought that *Penthouse* for the john at work. Went in the john 20 minutes later and saw someone threw it in the trash. It's sad how some people can't appreciate nice things.

FRIDAY, JUNE 10, 2011

Gonna hit up karaoke again tonight. Super pumped. Inviting EVERYONE. Gonna do some push-ups in the john. Gotta be jacked!

SATURDAY, JUNE 11, 2011

Karaoke was kind of a disaster. Invited Al, Dave, Ken, and Dave's buddy Crazy Cooter. Waited three hours to go up. Drank four 5-hour Energies.

Was supposed to sing Van Halen's "Jump," like I practiced for, but they played "Panama" instead. Tried to make up for my vocals with my moves. I was pretty bombed from the 5-hours and about ten Bacardi-and-Diets. Did some Diamond Dave spin kicks and knocked over the PA system. Fell off the stage and hurt my elbow pretty bad. The gal runnin' the karaoke got super steamed. Felt like a real assclown like Michael Anthony. I wasn't really kicked out, but they made me leave. Couldn't find my keys. They fell out of my pocket when I was doin' spin kicks. I had to BEG to go back in the bar and get my keys. Was on the floor lookin' for 'em and somebody spilled a whole beer on me. I started gettin' the spins from all the excitement. Felt like I was gonna pass out. Puked all over the floor. That's when I really got kicked out.

Think I waited by the 'Bring for the guys. Don't remember. Guess Dave found my keys though 'cause I woke up in the car this morning covered in dried beer and barf. They just left me there. Some kinda friends, huh?

Bacardi needs to make more realistic commercials. Have one where a grown man is blacked out in his Sebring, covered in puke and shame. I think I might really need to shape up, you guys. Might cut back to just brewskis for a while. Or vodka. Hear that's better for you.

9

DAD'S DAY AND CRAZY COOTER

JUNE 13–JULY 14, 2011

MONDAY, JUNE 13, 2011

Wonder what the kids have cooked up for Dad's Day? Should probably give 'em a ring. Been a few weeks. Communication is important, you guys.

This Father's Day, get Dad somethin' he really wants. Maybe a Callaway driver, a Kegerator, or shuttin' your mouth about him boozin' too much.

TUESDAY, JUNE 14, 2011

Got a "wrap" for lunch. It's like havin' a terrible burrito and a crappy sandwich all at the same time. Worst of both worlds. Healthy though. Stayin' strong, but it's tough. Keep cravin' pizza with mayo on it. Sometimes I can't decide whether I like Miracle Whip or mayo better. Miracle Whip has more flavor, but mayo is just such a classic. Could really go for some vitamin mayo right now. Feel light-headed.

WEDNESDAY, JUNE 15, 2011

Still wonder what Ann and the kids have planned for Dad's Day? Not returnin' my calls. Haven't talked in a while. Must be keepin' it hush-hush.

Hope Ann makes that German potato salad I like. It's ok to really indulge on Dad's Day when you've earned it, you guys. Maybe Ann's gonna grill some big juicy steaks? Sure would be nice to kick back and get waited on. Makes a dad really feel appreciated.

THURSDAY, JUNE 16, 2011

No word from Ann today about the big Dad's Day celebration. Must be busy preppin'. On Sunday, the Welzein clan must bow before King Karl!

Dave's eatin' José Olé burreets and drinkin' cold ones. Don't appreciate that while I'm tryin' to be good. Losers like him love to see other people fail. Sick of this. He's just disgusting. I'm goin' to eat this cottage cheese in the john.

FRIDAY, JUNE 17, 2011

You gotta fight! For your right! To Friiiiiidaaay! Really lookin' forward to the Dad's Day weekend. Dad's Day is one of those special holidays you want to spend with loved ones. Not like the 4th of July and other ones where they can get in the way of the party.

SATURDAY, JUNE 18, 2011

Still no word from Ann. Must be big, big, big! A surprise party maybe? Who knows? Super pumped. I mean, I'm sure it would never happen, but just once, I'd like for someone to give me a sports car with a bow on it as a gift.

SUNDAY, JUNE 19, 2011–DAD'S DAY

Haven't heard from Ann and the kids yet. Havin' a few cocktails. Who needs 'em anyway. It's DAD'S day, not FAMILY day. Nuts to them if they want to be crappy and thoughtless. Gonna treat myself to a nice Dad's Day pizza from Papa John's. Supreme, all the way. Pull out the stops. And I'm eatin' all the slices I want. Plus, I'm watchin' the US Open. Probably wouldn't have time to make small talk with the fam anyway. This is fine by me.

Double Crown-and-Diets are goin' down so smooth, you guys. Ann gives me the stink-eye when I get into the Crown. This is MY day.

4:45 P.M.

Did a few shotskis, Papa's in the house, US Open is rockin'. Might be the best Dad's Day ever. No need for that family time horsecrap. Just a tip for all you dads out there: Ditch the fam next year. You'll be glad ya did. I gotta mean buzz on and no one's yappin' their gums. Livin' the dream.

6:47 P.M.

Ann just rang! Wants to know where I am?! Said she told me about 6 p.m. supper last week. Musta been boozed or forgot to write it down. Guess she has steaks goin', chips, cold ones, the works! Full spread. I'm kinda too bombed to see good or drive and stuffed with 'za, but headin' over on Dave's ten-speed. The party's on!

1:15 A.M.

Wiped out pretty bad on Dave's ten-speed halfway to Ann's tonight. Messed up my jean shorts. Lyin' on the side of the road with a scraped-up knee, pukin' my guts out in the humidity, kinda made me feel like I was in 'Nam. Never been, but I'd imagine that kinda thing happened a ton.

Dave's ten-speed sucks. The chain falls off if it isn't in first gear, tires are almost completely flat, and the seat's crooked. My crotch got all chafed. Real raw and tender. Jean shorts and sweaty dampness don't mix with a crooked seat, you guys. Shoulda just drove. Got to Ann's an hour and a half late. Soaked with sweat and bleeding. Kinda badass? Feel like that's how a real man should enter a Dad's Day celebration. Too bad the steaks were all burned and cold. Plus, my greedy son pigged down all the Cool Ranch D'reets. At least the cold ones were still fine. Ann got the good stuff. Sam Adams is for special occasions. Goes down so smooth with bold flavors. She only got a 6-pack though. Who does that? For a Dad's Day celebration? Six brews? It's kind of a kick in the sack. If you have a party and only have a 6-pack of suds, it's not a party. It's just sayin', "You're not welcome and we'd like you to leave ASAP." I polished off the sixer, did a "no thanks" on the burned steak, and hit the bricks. I know where I'm not wanted.

The only present I got was what I thought was a "penis man" from my son. Turned out to be a magician. Straight in the trash.

Got sick of Dave's crappy bike on the way home. Threw it on the side of the road. Walked home in a lightning storm, prayin' to get lit up. Shoulda just stayed home with my 'za, Crown, and US Open. Never leave a party you're havin' a blast at to go to one your family's throwing you. Dad's Day would be the party of the year if dads got to spend it with people they like to party with instead of their families.

My inner thighs are so chafed from my wet jean shorts, I can hardly move. I have to walk like a big black gal. Jean shorts need to come with a warning: May cause extreme chafing if worn while wet or sweaty.

Dave's complainin' 'cause I threw his bike away on the side of the road. I've NEVER seen him ride it. Says I owe him money. What a scam artist. What's a crappy 1987 Murray ten-speed worth anyway? I did him a favor by takin' that trash out for him. If anything, Dave should thank me that he'll never have to ride that piece of crap again.

My crotch is so destroyed, you guys.

MONDAY, JUNE 20, 2011

Went to work for about an hour. Crotch was in such pain I had to leave. Also, threw up a few times. Think Ann got some expired Sam Adams. Probably on sale. Figures.

TUESDAY, JUNE 21, 2011

Wore swim trunks to work today because of my raw crotch. Nosey Lady seems to have a beef with it. Oh, like she's never had a raw crotch before. I told Nosey Lady to go on a two-mile bike ride in sweaty jean shorts and see how HER crotch feels! She shot me a look and wrote somethin' down. Then came back late to "inform" me that "crotch" isn't an appropriate term for work.

WEDNESDAY, JUNE 22, 2011

Startin' to feel better. Took the day off to soothe my raw crotch. Been just layin' here thinkin' 'bout gettin' the boat out this weekend. Really kick the summer off right. Cruisin', sippin' cold ones, wavin' at babes. Them wavin' back. Nothin' beats it. My son always gets sick on boats. It's kind of why I don't think we can ever be close. Boating is a really important part of my life.

SUNDAY, JUNE 26, 2011

Ate a load of crap on the golf course yesterday. Drank a buttload though. Felt like John Daly. Champs like him don't always have to "win."

Was takin' a whizz on the 7th hole and some fat a-hole and his old lady got all steamed about it. Idiot. Peein' and golf go together like brats and mustard. If there's one freedom left in this country, it's a man's right to take a leak on a golf course. I don't care if your gross wife is there. Who golfs with their wife anyway? Dave was pretty bombed and started makin' sow noises at her. Ha! The fat a-hole said he was going to tell management about our "behavior." I told him, "Suck it, pal." Thought his head was gonna explode! They just left without finishin' their round. Who does that? Guys who golf with their gross wife, that's who.

Man, we are still dyin' laughin' about it. Poundin' cold ones. Just keeps gettin' better and better with each brewski. Life's all about great stories, you guys.

MONDAY, JUNE 27, 2011

This is definitely a multiple toilet nap kinda Monday, you guys. Could sure go for a gun in my mouth. If every week was only Monday and Tuesday, over and over again, I'm 100% sure I'd gladly kill myself.

Feelin' just awful. Lunch break. Gonna go drink a couple cold ones in the Sebring at the 7-Eleven parkin' lot and catch a quick snooze.

2:45 P.M.

Woke up in the 'Bring soaked in sweat. Got in hot water for takin' a long lunch break. Told Nosey Lady I had to change a flat. Just because a diarrhea excuse always works, it doesn't mean you should use it every time. Variety is the spice of lies.

Really draggin'. Didn't eat lunch except for those two beers. Need a solid supper. Maybe Chili's. It's still healthy if you order careful. Heard they're havin' somethin' called the Margar-EAT-athon. Man, that is genius. Sometimes when you're feelin' down, wantin' to blow your brains out, out of nowhere, Chili's saves the day. Thanks, Chili's. Gonna swing by the pad and get cleaned up first. Got some pretty bad BO from snoozin' in the 'Bring. It's important to be fresh.

WEDNESDAY, JUNE 29, 2011

Really lookin' forward to the 4th, you guys. Might get the boat out. Really do it right. Gotta find my bottle rocket stash. Hope Ann doesn't have "family plans." She only lets us have sparklers. Nothin' says "my country, 'tis of thee" like shootin' bottle rockets out of a beer bottle on your boat while you're hammered for America. Nothin'.

I was grillin' brats as a warm-up for the 4th and Dave threw a whole fistful of those TNT Pop-Its at my back. Burned a bunch of little holes in my Corona tee! Sick of this.

There's two things everyone knows not to mess with: #1: Texas #2: Another man's Corona tee. Dave is gonna pay for that. I hope he likes it when I fire a whole gross of bottle rockets at him! Really steamed. That Corona tee was brand-new for the weekend. Just because Corona is an overpriced beer doesn't mean they don't make a stylin' T-shirt, you guys.

4:30 P.M.

Waitin' for Dave to use the john. Gonna crack the door, throw the bottle rockets in there, then hold the door shut. Gonna be a smooth move.

Revenge is a dish best served cold, as in when you've had nine or ten cold ones in the early afternoon, you guys.

4:55 P.M.

Dave just went in the can. He had five Cheddar Wursts so he should be in there a while. This is a real brown-ops mission. Ha!

5:20 P.M.

Oh my God. Went to throw the bottle rockets at Dave in the john. He had the door locked. Over a hundred went off in the hallway. Oh God. At least thirty bottle rockets must have exploded on me. Lots of small burns. Cargo shorts are ruined. Big patch gone out of my arm hair. Oh God.

The whole hallway is all covered in burns. Looks like a war zone. Smoke is so thick I can't breath. Ears are ringing so bad I wanna puke. This is ALL Dave's fault. WHAT KIND OF MAN LOCKS THE DOOR TO THE TOILET?! DOES HE PEE SITTING DOWN TOO?! If Dave thinks I'm cleaning this bottle rocket mess up, he is so wrong. This is all on him for ruining my nice Corona tee. He started it!

Dave came running out of the john with his pants down and peener out, screaming like a woman. What a baby. Guess he can't handle explosions.

The pad is pretty messed up. But you really haven't partied hard enough for the 4th if you didn't destroy at least one piece of furniture. Looks like a few bottle rockets made it to the couch. There's like six holes in it. But it was ruined anyway from where Dave sharted on it.

8:35 P.M.
Dave just called Aretha Franklin "Urethra Franklin." Ha! We had a guy-to-guy and everything's cool now.

SUNDAY, JULY 3, 2011

Today feels kinda like Christmas Eve except tomorrow's not gonna suck with church, crappy weather, and kids crying over dumb crap.

Christmas has one tree inside, sissy lights, and family time. The 4th has all the trees outside, fireworks, and cold ones. 4th for the win, all the way. The 4th is for AMERICA. For all our freedoms and hard work. Christmas is for one guy who did some nice stuff but really can't top the USA. Plus, I don't like how all the other filthy countries get to celebrate Christmas. The 4th is just for the Red, White, and Blue. This is OUR time.

Dave said his buddy Crazy Cooter is throwin' a backyard bash at his place tonight. Sounds like a blast. Headin' out soon.

MONDAY, JULY 4, 2011

For being 235 years old, America is one sweet-lookin' lady. Happy birthday to all my fellow Americans. Proud to be with ya, you guys.

Got pretty messed up on Crazy Cooter's jungle juice last night. Can't stop these spins. I'm gonna go lay down next to the toilet.

TUESDAY, JULY 5, 2011

Really hurtin' today, you guys. But if you don't feel like your brain is being dug out with an ice cream scoop, you didn't do the 4th right.

After I woke up from my nap by the toilet, me and Dave went back to Crazy Cooter's. Man, he keeps the party rockin' like a ZZ Top video.

Crazy Cooter is pretty much livin' the dream. He's got an aboveground pool and everything! Lives with his ma, but she stays out of the way.

Crazy Cooter made another batch of jungle juice. Think I'm gettin' used to it 'cause man, I was flyin' afterward and feelin' fine. Cannonballed into his pool holdin' a Roman candle. Wanted Dave to get a pic but I splashed him and kinda fried my digital camera. Idiot. He shoulda stood back farther. Let Crazy Cooter smash it with a mini-sledge. Seemed to make him happy so it wasn't a total waste.

Crazy Cooter just called Dave. Said we should come over with a few cold ones. This guy is a maniac! Gonna have one or two to be polite, then head to Ann's to smooth things over. She's steamed I didn't make it over yesterday. But hey, why should I ruin my holiday?

THURSDAY, JULY 7, 2011

Things got kinda weird at Crazy Cooter's last night. He showed us a pic of his lady and said, "She ain't much to look at, but she sure can fuck." Crazy Cooter has a thing or two to learn about babes.

Crazy Cooter ALWAYS wants to party, which is cool, but EVERY NIGHT can't be party night unless you're in Aerosmith or something. He started "dancing with the white lady" right in front of his ma. She didn't even care. Thought that was odd, you guys.

A little grass and cold ones are ok, but I learned a long time ago to say nope to dope unless you're just doin' a nummer to look cool.

Never made it over to Ann's. I think Crazy Cooter might be a bad influence.

FRIDAY, JULY 8, 2011

And I just can't fight this Friday anymorrrre! I've forgotten what I started work-in' forrrr!!! Happy Friday to ya, you guys.

Supposed to get the boat out of dry storage tomorrow. Can't wait! Cold ones, cruisin', jammin' out, sandwiches. Gonna be a blast. Might invite Ann and the kids. When you spend a lot of time with a violent cokehead named Crazy Cooter, it makes you appreciate your fam.

9:05 P.M.

Saw Ann tonight. Said she's carrying six almonds for when she's hungry like Oprah. I told her, "Oprah looks like she carries six pizzas." Ha! Ann said, "That's not very nice to say about Oprah."

Oprah can suck it. She ruined my marriage with her bullcrap. Probably a lot of others too.

SATURDAY, JULY 9, 2011

Boat time! Boat, boat, boat! Ann and the kids aren't comin' 'cause I couldn't find the kids' life jackets. So stupid. Why did I pay for swimming lessons?! Bringin' Dave. He can't swim at all and isn't wearin' a life jacket. Told him he couldn't. Looks weak to the lake babes.

SUNDAY, JULY 10, 2011

Had a blast yesterday. Until we ran out of gas. Me and Dave had to just sit there with our thumbs up our butts for three hours. Boat gauges must be off. Had to wait for a service to come and bring us fuel. Ran out of sandwiches too. It was a nightmare. Drank all the cold ones while we waited for gas. The guy gave us looks for bein' bombed. Like you have to be sober to drive a boat. Idiot. I was tryin' to get that rich cocoa tan so I just put on baby oil. So sunburned now that I keep gettin' the chills. Hope it just turns into a nice base.

Feel kinda delirious. Can't stop laughing about what a great stripper name "Aloe Vera" would be for a cocoa honey.

MONDAY, JULY 11, 2011

This sunburn is killin' me. Hurts to move. Ken said, "Hey, Kool-Aid! Get some sun there, buddy?" Wasn't necessary to hurt my feelings too.

No one makes fun of Guy Fieri when he gets a little extra sun. Havin' a rich cocoa tan is just part of the bold flavor lifestyle, you guys.

People always say how Fonzie is the king of cool, but I bet if he saw Guy Fieri comin', he'd be shakin' in his shoes. And if Guy Fieri ever teamed up with Papa John, they'd pretty much be unstoppable.

Just a tip from Karl: If you're driving a convertible, a backward Kangol is a must-have for the summertime, you guys. It pretty much goes with anything from jean shorts to cargo jean shorts, and classes up ANY tank, golf shirt, or Big Dogs tee.

TUESDAY, JULY 12, 2011

One of my co-workers (can't say who) got caught watching porno at work today. Ken is in so much trouble! (It was Ken.)

Pretty much the best thing that can happen at work on a Tuesday is a co-worker gettin' caught watchin' porno. That or a free pizza lunch. Both are the best.

Wonder what kinda porno Ken is into? Never was much for that hard-core action myself. I like to leave a little to the imagination, you guys. Sure, I've always enjoyed a nice *Penthouse*. It's a gentlemen's read. There's a big difference between porno and tasteful nudity.

WEDNESDAY, JULY 13, 2011

Thinkin' about headin' down to see Steely Dan on Saturday. Really chill out, you guys. "The Cuervo Gold, the fine Colombian . . ." What a jam.

THURSDAY, JULY 14, 2011

Really lookin' forward to the weekend, you guys.

10

THE HEAT IS ON

JULY 15-27, 2011

FRIDAY, JULY 15, 2011

Really lookin' forward to the weekend, you guys. Heard that new Harry Potter crap is comin' out. This is always a good time for anyone with a kid to start havin' "back problems." Really juice it. Lots of layin' down on the floor in pain. Really go Larry Bird on a timeout with it. Always worked for Larry gettin' outta listenin' to some coach tellin' him some crap he didn't need to hear, and it works just as fine to get out of seein' some movie you don't wanna see. Was Larry Bird faking? Guess we'll never know.

Whatever happened to GOOD movies like *Beverly Hills Cop II?* Action, babes, guns, tons of laughs. It's a real quality film with a good message: If you mess around in the USA with your sleazy crime schemes, you're goin' down. Harry Potter's such a bad influence. It makes kids have dreams that'll never come true.

Dave likes Harry Potter. He bought all the books to look cool but just watched the movies and acts like he read 'em. Yeah, that'll get babes. "Hey, gal, look at my collection of children's magic books. Let's get carnal." Such a turnoff. Real creepy. If you're gonna have a bunch of books you pretend to read, at least pick up some John Grishams or other intellectual crap. Even if you're a bad boy, it shows you have some class and might be about to make a power move in life.

I think it's kinda weird that no one's made a buddy cop action flick with Guy Fieri in it yet. It'd be a summer smash at the box office. Probably sweep the nation. Seems so simple. I'm gonna ditch out of work for a bit, have a few cold ones in the 7-Eleven parking lot, and work out this idea. Gotta have priorities, you guys.

* BOLD WEAPON
(FILM BY KARL WELZEIN) *

SCOTT BOLD (GUY FIERI) IS A RENEGADE COP WHO MOONLIGHTS AS A CHEF, AND HAS A WEAKNESS FOR CARNAL PASSIONS WITH EROTIC BABES. SICK OF BEING JUDGED AT THE DEPARTMENT FOR HIS ROCK 'N ROLL LIFESTYLE, HE DECIDES TO GO ON THE LAM TO TAKE DOWN THE ORIENTAL CARTEL, HIS WAY, IN THE BOLD BOY STYLE. TEAMING UP WITH JAMAL HOLIDAY, A SMOOTH HUSTLER FROM THE STREETS WHO'S ALSO SICK OF THE ORIENTAL CARTEL GETTIN IN HIS BUSINESS AFFAIRS. (JAMAL COULD BE PLAYED BY PRETTY MUCH ANY BLACK FUNNYMAN. I HAVE ANOTHER LIST BUT WOULD LIKE TO ADD ON CEDRIC THE ENTERTAINMENT) THEY KICK ASS ON EVERYONE WITH MOVES FROM MARTIAL ARTS, BOXING, AND WWF. AT THE END, SCOTT BOLD GETS SO STEAMED THAT HE JUST BLOWS UP CHINATOWN, 'CAUSE HE HAD NO OTHER CHOICE. SADDENED, HE LEAVES TOWN. WILL THE WORLD SEE SCOTT BOLD AGAIN?
* MAYBE IN BOLD WEAPON 2. *

SATURDAY, JULY 16, 2011

Super pumped. Headin' down to the Steely Dan show tonight. It's gonna be so money. Me, Dave, and Al. Just gonna pregame with a few cold ones and smoke a little grass maybe. (Definitely. Ha!) Guess we're just gonna try to score some tickets when we get there. Shouldn't be too hard. It's not like a Nuge show where everybody's ragin' to see the Motor City Madman. It's more of a mellow vibe. I made a big Thermos of G&Ts for the trip. It's ok to drink and drive when you're goin' to see a concert in Detroit. Takes the edge off. Get back, jack, do it agaaaiin! Puttin' the top down on the 'Bring. Let's do this!

SUNDAY, JULY 17, 2012

Really hurtin' today, you guys. Steely D was a disaster. As soon as we got there, I scored some Rice Krispy Treats (with weed in 'em). I ate two because I was starving. Two was too many. Way too many. We wandered around tryin' to find tickets but I guess Steely D is still pretty popular. Didn't know. Dave and Al were bein' cheapskates and wouldn't buy tickets because they were too expensive so they just went to a bar. It looked pretty cool, but I couldn't let down Steely D, so I had to go in by myself.

I ended up spendin' the whole show in the john stall. Had a freak-out and didn't want to get off the pot. Talk about 175 bucks down the toilet. After the show, I was still pretty tripped out and couldn't find Dave, Al, or the Sebring. And I forgot my cell in the car. I wandered around the same four blocks in Detroit until 4 a.m. So the drugs were probably a good idea after all, otherwise it might have been a pretty dark experience.

When I finally found the Sebring with Dave and Al in it, they were passed out, covered in trash. Guess we forgot to put the top up in all the excitement. And it looked like somebody urinated on

Dave. All the filthy animals in Detroit should be locked up so responsible adults can enjoy a nice time without having their friends urinated on.

I think there's still some of that weed in my system. I just don't feel right. Wish Dave would wake up and talk to me. Could really use a guy-to-guy. Maybe I'll call Ann? She always knew how to talk me down.

Could really use her touch. Gonna go outside to get some air.

The Sebring looks pretty rough. On the way home this morning, Dave tried to throw up outta the car when we were goin' 60 on I-75. Real disaster. Real classic Dave. 90-degree weather, urine, fast food trash, and puke do not mix well with the interior of a Chrysler. It's like we brought Detroit home with us.

WEDNESDAY, JULY 20, 2011

Happy Wing Wednesday! Took out 18 Caribbean Jerks. They have the bold island spices I crave. Sometimes you need to take a step back from your diet or your bod gets too used to it. Then, when you get back on that horse, the lbs. just melt off.

It's so hot out today. The AC at work started to slow down, then finally just conked out. I couldn't stand it anymore, so I went down to my undertank and hit the john where it's nice and cool. I could only stay in there for a little bit though 'cause Ken was rankin' it up pretty bad. I tried to make small talk, but it felt weird with my shirt off and his pants down at the same time.

I finally just asked Nosey Lady if we could leave for the day, but she said no. I think she wears that organic deodorant crap, 'cause her BO was comin' on strong enough for a man but made for a man. In this kinda heat, she might as well just wear BO-scented deodorant.

When I got home I made a big pitcher of vodka lemonade,

turned the AC on full blast, and put a box fan blastin' at my crotch. Here's a little beat-the-heat tip from Captain Karl: Go heavy with Gold Bond on your plumbing, then let a box fan cool your boys down like Dalton from *Road House*. But when beatin' the heat with Gold Bond, don't beat your meat. Dave had a disaster situation on his hands last summer. Ha!

THURSDAY, JULY 21, 2011

Really lookin' forward to the weekend, you guys.

I beat the heat AND kept it healthy today with the Arby's Cool Deli Sandwich. Health tip: Cold sandwiches are lower in cals than the oven-baked ones. Heat brings out the oils and fats.

I should've just hung out at Arby's all day. The AC was blasting, and I could pretty much just soak in that Arby's aroma forever. They should make bathroom air fresheners like Arby's smell, Beer Brat smell, or Supreme Pizza smell. Only gals should cover up their BMs with lilacs.

Wore my swim trunks today 'cause of the heat. If Nosey Lady has a problem with that, it's easy access to kiss my sweaty butt. Had a problem this afternoon though. I was pushin' out a long Arby's stinky in the john and my legs stuck to the seat. When I tried to stand up, I crashed back down and broke the toilet tank lid. Again. Sometimes mistakes happen twice, especially when they're not your fault. I'm NOT paying for it. No AC at work makes it hazardous to use the toilet. It's like makin' #2 in a third-world country, if they were lucky enough to have Arby's.

FRIDAY, JULY 22, 2011

Carry on, my Friday son! There'll be drinks when you are done. Lay your weary head to rest! Don't you work no more! Happy Friday, you guys!

We had a meeting today about the broken toilet tank lid. Nosey Lady is all steamed. I already lied about breaking it once the last time, so twice should be a breeze. She wanted me to sign something that says I didn't break the toilet tank lid, so I signed it. Besides, it's ok to lie about destroying property when you did it 'cause of the heat.

So sick of this broken AC. If I can make it through the day, I'm drinkin' so many top-shelf margs it'll make Jimmy Buffett look like a 3rd grade girl. It's just so hot. I'm going to get a Gatorade. And put booze in it. And drink it at work. Because screw this bullcrap. It's Friday. MY day.

SATURDAY, JULY 23, 2011

Kept it cool all night with 'Cardi-and-Gatorade, the RESPONSIBLE summer bev. It keeps you hydrated AND keeps the party rockin' 'til you black out.

They should market 'Cardi-and-Gatorade. Think I'd be a great spokesman.

Captain Karl here for 'Cardi-and-Gatorade. 'Cardi-and-Gatorade— you won't remember much after 10 p.m., that's the 'Cardi-and-Gatorade promise.

Woke up this mornin' and started back in with the 'Cardi-and-Gatorade, and boy, am I hammered already again, you guys.—Captain Karl

Hi, I'm Captain Karl. MY special recipe for 'Cardi-and-Gatorade? Take a big tumbler. Add ice. Dump a bunch of 'Cardi and Gatorade in it. Pound accordingly.

I should really talk to someone about these ideas. They're great. I'd get the boat out today to celebrate if it wasn't so crappy. I'd drive the shit outta that thing right now. 'Cardi-and-Gatorade got me feelin' good!

Haven't talked to Ann in a while. I don't think she loves me anymore. Wish she'd reach out. I got so much to tell her that she's missin' out on.

MONDAY, JULY 25, 2011

Because no one fessed up to the broken toilet tank lid that I broke, now we have to ask for a key from Nosey Lady to use the john. It's such a nightmare. I'm on a special diet. I have to use the john more than most people. I need 24/7 access to that toilet. I can't be bothered to ask Nosey Lady for a key every time. Plus, she'll know how long I've been in the john when I give the key back. Sometimes I need a quick snooze. Who doesn't?

If it comes down to me filling my pants with stool or kickin' down the door to the locked john, I'm kickin' that door down like Steven Seagal.

I knew what would happen. It got to be way past time for my 5 p.m. BM and Nosey Lady wasn't around anywhere with the john key. My stomach started to really hurt, so I did it. I went #2 behind the Dumpster at work. Used some Burger King napkins for cleanup. Is this what my life has come to? Sick of this.

TUESDAY, JULY 26, 2011

Turned in my complaint about the locked john first thing.

Stayed late at work to see if there was any response to my complaint. NOTHING. I might have to take drastic measures. This will not stand! You don't mess with a man's toilet privileges.

To Whom It May Concern,

Yesterday, July25, 2011, the employees of ██████████ were told that they would be required to ask for a restroom key from ██████ in order to use the john for urinating or defecation purposes. This was implemented due to the fact that "someone" broke the toilet tank lid. Who was that "someone?" Sadly, I guess we'll never know. Must be someone with no class. Unfortunately, now we're all being punished for it.

Adults should be free to use the john as they please, whether it be to relieve themselves, or check their appearance in the mirror to make sure that their hair or make up is just right. It's important to be presentable. I personally take great pride in my appearance. That's why I am on a special diet that keeps me lean and fit. This special diet also has its drawbacks, such a frequent restroom breaks.

Yesterday, I enjoyed a healthy salad from Burger King, and after it digested, I felt the need to purge it from my body, which is natural. Sadly, when that time came, ██████, the keeper of the key to the john was nowhere to be found. I did my very best to hold in my waste but after 5 to 10 minutes, it became an impossibility.

Concerned that I would defecated on myself, I was forced to exit the building and use the facilities, as they say, behind the dumpster in the rear parking lot. Luckily, I had a good number of Burger King napkins left over from my lunch break as I always ask for extras. I like to keep things tidy, but sadly, those napkins were used for something other than cleaning Ken's LITE Ranch dressing off of my shirt or car seat. It was humiliating, and I feel saddened by this event.

In order to avoid similar future incidents, I move that the men's john be returned to it's previous unlocked state, free for all to enjoy.

This was a horrible experience for me, but perhaps it can be used for good, so that no one else has to defecate behind the work dumpster like a common street person. Remember, it could happen to any of you.

Thank you for your time. Regards,

KARL WELZEIN

arl Welzein

Snuck into the ladies' room last night and took a MONSTER BM, then clogged the toilet really good with TP. Told everyone Nosey Lady did it. She's all steamed about it, but that just made her look more suspicious. Everyone knows, she who smelt it clogged it. When someone starts a toilet war, you can just call me Rambo, you guys.

In the afternoon, Nosey Lady informed me that they wanted to have a meeting with me about my complaint letter. Thought it was time for justice, so I tape-recorded the whole thing in case I wanted to play it back at a victory party later. Here's what they fed me:

We understand that you became upset with our policy on restroom usage. However, it is incomprehensible how a grown man could be driven to defecate in public behind his place of work because he had to wait just ten minutes for a restroom key.

While we aren't forcing you to do so, you may want to consult a therapist as this is not acceptable behavior in society.

As far as your employment is concerned, there really is no reference point for us to go from at this time as no employee has defecated on the company's property in any place other than a restroom. Also, please know what you did was illegal.

Unfortunately, Karl, we have no other choice but to suspend you from work for one week, with pay, until we can sort out the situation.

Sorry to curse, it's not my style, but fuck those assholes. I'm going to Paddy's. Sick of this.

11

CAPTAIN KARL'S PIZZA SHIP

JULY 28-AUGUST 4, 2011

THURSDAY, JULY 28, 2011

When you're suspended from work with pay, every day is the weekend. I haven't been treated fairly, but it could be worse. I'm gonna really take advantage of my time off. Can't let a moment go to waste. This might be my time to make a big life change. There's a lot of projects I need to finish up. First off is my restaurant idea for Captain Karl's Pizza Ship.

I went to the store for some markers, cold ones, and a dry-erase board. With a whole week off, Captain Karl's Pizza Ship could be a go. Then I'd never have to go back to that hellhole. Really shove it in their face.

Before any big project, you gotta have a snack. Gives you brain energy. I went for some Triscuits and mayo. Such a winning combination. When I was a kid, I always had Triscuits and mayo after school. Now they have off-the-hook flavors like Rosemary & Olive Oil. It's a modern twist on a classic from way back.

Health tip: Just because you're laid off from work, you can't let your diet go out the window. Skip the chips and dip, and keep it in the health zone with Triscuits and LOW-FAT mayo.

This business plan is lookin' really on point. So money.

THE RULES OF CAPTAIN KARL'S PIZZA SHIP (OUR MOTTO)

Rule #1 of Captain Karl's Pizza Ship: You can get Cheetos on ANYTHING for an extra dollar. (Guy Fieri would come by in a second on this alone.)

Rule #2 of Captain Karl's Pizza Ship: ONLY handicrapper-sized stalls. EVERYONE is special at Captain Karl's.

Rule #3 of Captain Karl's Pizza Ship: Complimentary Triscuits and mayo when you're seated. An old treat from the Seven Seas!

Rule #4 of Captain Karl's Pizza Ship: No vegan fake meat and cheese crap. This ain't Captain Hippie's Soy Trash Barge for Sissies.

Rule #5 of Captain Karl's Pizza Ship: Our sandwiches are served "piled high" with your choice of fries or Captain Karl's Mashed and Country Gravy.

Rule #6 of Captain Karl's Pizza Ship: Only C- to DD-cup sea wench waitresses. Like Hooters but less trashy. And NO dude waiters.

Quittin' time. The best part about bein' laid off is YOU'RE the boss. Headin' to cold one city, and it's well earned, I might add.

FRIDAY, JULY 29, 2011

Woke up this morning and saw Dave hung a pair of wet underpants on my dry-erase board notes for Captain Karl's Pizza Ship. He doesn't know anything about business. And I don't want to know anything about why his underpants were all wet. Threw 'em in the trash.

Started my day off with a cold one and an egg sandwich. Bein' your own boss is the high life. Dave has the day off too, but it looks like the only thing he's the boss of is watchin' *Caddyshack II* at a terrible volume. Is that all he does on his days off? He doesn't understand that I work for myself now so I can't just dick around. I gotta chase my dream! Captain Karl's Pizza Ship* takes focus. Most people are happy just havin' a 9-to-5 or cleanin' toilets at the gas station. That's never been my style.

Rule #7 of Captain Karl's Pizza Ship: On summer weekends, shirt and shoes are optional. It'll be like an island paradise with comfortable sandy floors.

Rule #8 of Captain Karl's Pizza Ship: Whiskey and a Wing Wednesday. Get a shot of Jack and a Buffalo Wing for just 3 bucks!

Rule #9 of Captain Karl's Pizza Ship: Over-the-Top Tuesdays. Arm-wrestling tournament and 50-cent Busch drafts all night long!

Dave won't stop buggin' me to watch *Caddyshack II* with him. Yes, I know it's hilarious, but I'm tryin' to build a restaurant empire here. If everyone had my level of focus and didn't spend so much time screwin' off on the computer or watchin' the boob tube, the world would be a better place.

Holy crap! I just saw that today is National Chicken Wing Day! Goin' to BW3's! Even MLK would take time off from his dream for such a celebration, you guys.

---

* Mental Note: I gotta get one of those Countdown to St. Paddy's Day digital signs for Captain Karl's Pizza Ship. That's how you know a place is a rockin' joint.

I feel so empty without a job. I wonder what Ann's up to? She could probably use a call from ol' Karl. It'd really give her a thrill.

Dave's watchin' SummerSlam wrestling on pay-per-view. Guess who's gonna end up payin' for it again? Me. Hope it's not more than 5 bucks. I decided to check it out though. Haven't watched it for a while. Used to be a big fan in the Stone Cold Steve Austin days. I'm really into this new CM Punk guy. He comes out to "Cult of Personality." It's such a hard rock jam. And he means business. Looks like he'd give Dalton from *Road House* a run for his money. And that's really saying somethin'.

My favorite guy that's still around might be Triple H. He's perty badass. Triple H has a ROCKIN' ponytail. It kinda makes me sad that I haven't thought about growin' a ponytail 'til now. I gotta start eatin' Jell-O. Heard it makes your hair grow faster. The quicker I get a ponytail, the quicker I get to Babe City, USA. A rockin' ponytail isn't just about looks, it's about confidence. If Guy Fieri had a ponytail, he'd probably blow Kevin Costner out of the water for *People* magazine's Sexiest Man of the Year.

I decided I'd get an earring to tide me over 'til my pony grows in. Dave told me he could totally do it. I only trust him 'cause it can't be too hard. Numbed my ear up with ice and did a few shots of Jim Beam. Seemed like the cowboy thing to do. Like in the Old West. Dave started to stick the needle through, but halfway, he started to get sick and barfed all over my best jean shorts. I got really steamed and just did it myself. Guess my strength is more than I realize, and mixed with my anger and the Jimmer, the needle went clean through and into my neck. Hurt like a bastard, but I guess that's the high price of cool.

The real problem was that we didn't have an earring to put through the hole. The only dude we knew that probably had one was Crazy Cooter, so I piled some TP on my bloody neck and headed over. Crazy Cooter hooked me up with a riotous dangly cross earring. It's badass, but I'm gonna eventually have to swap it for a hoop. Just looks more professional. A gold hoop is such a classic.

I can't sleep. My ear's hurtin' bad from the piercing. I think Dave really botched it. Also, I shoulda cleaned the earring from Crazy Cooter before I put it in, but I didn't wanna look like a siss. Gonna soak my ear in rubbing alcohol, pound a few cold ones, and try to catch a few z's.

MONDAY, AUGUST 1, 2011

Man, they're gonna flip when I come back to work with this cool-ass earring. "Is that Guy Fieri or Karl?! I can't tell?!" Real bad boy.

Dave had a great idea for Captain Karl's Pizza Ship today: Ranch Corn Nut Pizza. Oh, did I say "great"? I meant "stupid." He's such a doofus. Ranch Corn Nuts are swell by themselves, but someone could lose a tooth on one, then it's lawsuit time. Or someone could choke to death, then who's gonna take care of the dead body? Sure as shit ain't gonna be Dave. Cheetos are a better topping option. That's why I'M the mastermind.

TUESDAY, AUGUST 2, 2011

Called up Ann. She said I can stop by for supper tonight. We'll see if she notices my new 'rang. It'd really make her feel bummed for all the bad boy stuff she's missin' out on. She never wanted me to get one, but I bet she changes her tune when she sees my sex appeal.

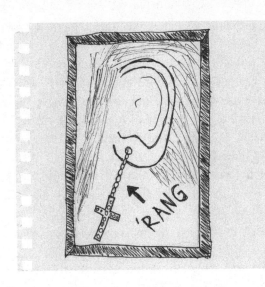

WEDNESDAY, AUGUST 3, 2011

I went to Ann's for supper last night. She didn't get into my new 'rang like I thought. Or at least she didn't act like it. Probably just jealous of my rock 'n' roll lifestyle. Everyone was really quiet at supper so I asked, what's up? They started crackin' up. Ann said, "An earring?! Is that a clip-on? Look out, everyone, it's Renegade!" Like she doesn't LOVE Lorenzo Lamas on that show. She has every episode taped on VHS. My son asked, "Is Daddy a girl now?" He's such a stupid idiot. It's an EARRING. Most badass dudes have one. He's got a lot to learn about the world.

Stone Cold Steve Austin? Earring. Renegade? Earring. Dog the Bounty Hunter? Earring. Michael Jordan? Earring. Guy Fieri? Earring. A 'rang lets the world know you kick ass and take names like I do. I told my son, "Know who DOESN'T have an earring? Harry friggin' Potter."

Got some more work done on the 'Za Ship. It's lookin' so money:

Rule #10 of Captain Karl's Pizza Ship: If you drink 11 Captain Karl's Top-Shelf Margs, 12 is on the Captain. (Only applies to the first 11.)

<u>POSSIBLE SLOGANS FOR CAPTAIN KARL'S PIZZA SHIP</u>
At Captain Karl's Pizza Ship, you'll stuff your gills without walking the plank.

Captain Karl's Pizza Ship: It's the finest grub from the Seven Seas and none of that guido crap. That's a promise. (Put this in the "maybe" pile. Might be too edgy.)

Captain Karl's Pizza Ship: Bold eats, top-shelf margs, and sweet babes' cans. (Needs a rewrite, but it's gettin' there.)

Dave thinks I should call it "Kaptain Karl's" instead of "Captain Karl's." I'm not some rapper. Don't wanna bring in the wrong crowd.

I think my work suspension was up today. I didn't know if I was supposed to go back. No one called though, and it's a paid suspension so I'm not in a rush. I might head to the bank with my Captain Karl's Pizza Ship notes in the a.m. If I can get a loan, work can kiss me where the sun don't shine. If you achieve your dreams, it's ok to really shove it in everyone's face. Even if they seemed supportive, they were probably lying. There were a lot of people who never thought I could get this cool earring. Now I'm the man, and they can suck it. What's next for me? Could be a chain wallet. Could be a ponytail. Who knows? What I DO know is I'm gonna keep rockin' 'n' rollin'. I just gotta be me and let nature do the rest.

THURSDAY, AUGUST 4, 2011

Just got back from the bank. The manager at that branch is a real assclown who clearly knows nothing about exciting business ventures.

I told him all about how Captain Karl's Pizza Ship would be all about top-shelf margs, Cheeto toppings, and babes' cans. He said he didn't "get it." I got really steamed. When I told him about the complimentary Triscuits and mayo, he looked like he was gonna laugh. I almost crushed his big-shot face in.

The bank manager said he was concerned that I never owned a restaurant before. What's to know except bold flavors, value booze, and busty sea wench waitresses? Then he told me that he thought "buy 11, get 1 free" top-shelf margs was "dangerous." What does THAT mean? How can a good value be "dangerous"? I think he had a problem with my 'rang. Squares never like to help out a rebel with a dream.

I finally felt so insulted that I stood up at his desk and told him how when I get Captain Karl's Pizza Ship up and going I'd be there to shove it in his face and take his wife out for the hottest date she's ever had. That's when the security guard escorted me out. I told him I wasn't some animal and I'd go quietly. I have class.

When I got in the Sebring in the parking lot, I cranked up the Nuge's "Stranglehold" and wailed on the gas like I was gonna plow through the window. Had to get it on. The bank manager came outside, so I psyched him out like he was gonna get run down with the

'Bring. I gave him the finger high and hard, then peeled out. Man, he was shakin' in his shoes.

To be fair, I probably shouldn't have had four Crown-and-Diets before my bank loan meeting, but I wanted to be loose and conversational.

Screw goin' back to work today. I'm goin' back Monday on MY terms. Gonna go to Chili's and cool off. If you're feelin' blue and in a psychotic rage, nothin' brings you back to normal like a nice afternoon at Chili's, you guys. Always hits the spot.

12

VERNON

AUGUST 10-22, 2011

WEDNESDAY, AUGUST 10, 2011

I'm kinda bummin' today that my earring hasn't made me any new friends or broken any babes' hearts. Makes me wonder if I'm cut out for the rock 'n' roll lifestyle. Or, maybe I just need to crank it up with TWO 'rangs, like Guy Fieri. He must be crushin' babes left and right. And if there's one thing I'm sure about, it's that Guy Fieri is one cool daddio with babes all around the world.

THURSDAY, AUGUST 11, 2011

Really lookin' forward to the weekend, you guys.

They hired a new black fella at work. Pretty cool. He's got an earring too, just like me. Might have to buddy up. Really take on the man. Guess his name's Vernon. And man, his style is so on point. Black mock turtleneck, pleated khaki slacks, mustache, and a 'rang? Such a winning combination. Looks so silky smooth. Just asked if he wanted to sneak out for an Arby's Jamocha Shake break. He said he's "a'ight." Vernon's so chillin', you guys.

I wonder if Vernon likes the Commodores? Bet he does. I like the Commodores too. I should ask him. We could chill and get funky sometime.

Think I'm gonna wear my Kangol tomorrow. Make Vernon feel welcome, like he's not the only funky soul brother at work. I always did pride myself in makin' newcomers feel welcome. Plus, if I teamed up with the new black guy at work, no one's gonna mess with us. When a white guy teams up with a black guy, anything is possible. Shoots-outs, adventures, tons of laughs, foxy cocoa honeys . . . anything.

Better hit the sack. Super pumped for Friday. Can't wait to kick it with Vernon. He seems pretty a'ight.

FRIDAY, AUGUST 12, 2011

Asked Vernon what the haps were for the weekend. He said, "Probably hittin' the club." Asked if me and Dave could join him. Vernon said, "A'ight." Super pumped. Never been to the club before! Vernon said he'd "hit me up" with a text when "him and his boys" head out.

Dave asked if he could wear his cargo shorts to the club. Idiot. If that's what he wants to do, he can just stay home. Dave can be so embarrassing. I'm wearing my silk shirt and goin' heavy on the 'logne. Man, can't wait to show off my dance moves. I'm sure folks are gonna appreciate the classics like "The Robot" and "The Worm." Gonna get down and funky fresh.

We're pregamin' with some orange-pop-and-Hennessy. Hear that's what the brothers crave to get pumped for the club. Don't know when Vernon's gonna "hit me up." Probably just gonna keep a solid buzz goin' all night to be ready. Kinda worried Dave might be overdoin' it though, he just did a shot of Hennessy. Good luck hurlin' later.

SATURDAY, AUGUST 13, 2011

Don't know how I'm gonna face Vernon on Monday, you guys.

Showed up at the club about 12:30. Me and Dave were pretty

bombed. Everyone seemed in a "Me So Horny" vibe, so I got right into it. Vernon said, "Yo, Karl, get your groove on." I didn't want to embarrass him, so I "got busy" on a caramel honey's big bootie. She had those long hair dread things. Turned out to be his homeboy named Darryl. It looked like cocoa babe from behind. Real disaster. Dave freaked out, screamin', "KARL, IS THIS A BLACK HOMO BAR?!" That's when I had a panic attack and puked all over Darryl's back.

I've pretty much decided that I can't bring Dave around my soul brother pals anymore. He needs to learn that screamin' "BLACK HOMO BAR" isn't cool. We got hauled out, and the bouncer hit Dave in the stomach for the "black homo" comment. He needed it. What an ass.

"Black homos" or not, you can't call gays "homos," regardless of skin color or whether they're gay or not. It's 2011. Plus, if anyone's a homo, it's Dave. Not that it's cool to say that. Whenever you feel the need to say "homo," try "jerk" if it's an insult or "gay" if it's just the facts. And sure, I might've puked up orange-pop-and-Hennessy all over Darryl's back when I dirty danced him, but I ain't a homophobe. It was just nerves.

MONDAY, AUGUST 15, 2011

Just hung out in the john most of the day. Vernon wouldn't talk to me at all. Just kept lookin' away and suckin' his teeth. Hope he doesn't give me a beat-down.

I think I'm getting anxiety attacks over the whole thing. Heart's racing. Diarrhea won't stop. I'm such a stupid idiot. I coulda just been chill and Vernon woulda thought I was cool. Now I'm just some dumb honky who pukes at the club like a clown. Sometimes I worry that I'm gonna die alone in that dump with Dave, without ever havin' any cool black friends or anything.

I got this damn earring. No one cares. I dress cool. No one cares. I'm a top-notch cook. No one cares. Sick of this. No one appreciates me. I'm sick of this stupid job. I never get to take my boat out. I never get to go golfing. I never get to do anything good. What's the damn point?

TUESDAY, AUGUST 16, 2011

Left Vernon a $20 Red Lobster gift card on his desk this morning. No "thank you" though. Guess some people are too cool to say "thanks" like the Fonz. If Fonzie was black, bet his coolness woulda been really off the hook. Probably woulda had a few kids though.

Made it through the whole workday without Vernon giving me a beat-down, so I guess the Red Lob gift card musta done the trick. Might start carrying one on me just in case for emergencies.

I shouldn't have to live this way. Gotta get my life together. Gonna go drink a few cold ones in the Sebring for some time to think. Maybe start smokin' cigs again on the regular to relax. I need to make better decisions.

WEDNESDAY, AUGUST 17, 2011

All that talk about Red Lobster yesterday had me cravin' some bold flavors from the Seven Seas. Saw it was Crabfest (only for a limited time) and had to take advantage with my first mate, Dave. When Red Lobster does it big with Crabfest, you don't think twice about it. Crabfest was off the hook. I had the Snow Crab and Roasted Garlic Seafood Bake for just $19.99. Dave got the Crab Linguini Alfredo but only used it for dippin' Cheddar Bay Biscuits into. Ate four baskets and took home his entrée for lefties. Smart move. Plus, we musta had six Lobsteritas each. It's Red Lob's version of the classic marg. They went down so smooth and were just a perfect pairing with their Crabfest selections.

I kept freakin' out that I saw Vernon at Red Lobster, but it always turned out to be some other black guy in a mock turtleneck with an earring. It's a timeless look for the brothers, and never goes out of style.

Red Lob is more of a weekend treat, but I felt like I earned it with everything that's been goin' on lately. When I was little, my family couldn't afford cafeteria food, and sometimes I'd only get a mustard sandwich in my lunch that I'd eat alone because I didn't have any friends. I'd cry every day after school 'cause I didn't have any pals except for my bro Al. Sometimes my mom would cry too 'cause we were poor. So that's why now, when I want Red Lobster on a Tuesday with my buddy Dave, I get Red Lobster. Makes a man feel like he made something of himself.

My mom was pretty much always workin' at some crap job or another. Never understood how she could spend so much time at work but still be poor. Sometimes I blamed her and thought she was just greedy. When I got older and realized that she was probably barely makin' enough for her, let alone three of us, I felt bad, like I shoulda helped out more. By then, she was gone though. Wish I coulda treated my mom to some Red Lob, you guys.

FRIDAY, AUGUST 19, 2011

Weekend wasteland! It's only weekend wasteland! Weekend wasteland, oh yeah!! WE'RE ALL WASTED!!! Happy Friday to ya, you guys.

Heard Guy Fieri is going to the Tigers game today. Gonna see if Dave and my bro Al wanna crew up and go. Might meet the man!

Pretty sure if Guy and the Triple D gang hooked up with the

Welzein boys, it'd be a bold flavor and cold one explosion for the books. Screw this. Gonna try and get out of work early. Gotta get down to Comerica. Might be my chance to tell Guy about Captain Karl's Pizza Ship. When you meet Guy Fieri, you have to play it cool. Elvis never made pals with dudes who acted like a little girl when they shook his hand. I'm pretty sure if I could just get some one-on-one time with Guy Fieri, my life would change forever. He has it all figured out.

SATURDAY, AUGUST 20, 2011

Yesterday was a nightmare. Tigers game was all jam-packed. Musta been because Guy Fieri was there. We had to scalp tickets. I forked over 300 bucks to some buffoon. Told us they were field-level tickets. Turned out to be standing room.

Couldn't find Guy Fieri anywhere at the Tigers game. He musta been in a box with all his fat-cat Triple D buddies, livin' the good life.

There's no way they'd let a superstar of the bold flavor world like Guy Fieri sit in normal seats at a big league game. He'd get mobbed.

We decided to just enjoy the game anyway, even if we couldn't meet Guy. Plus, there were a buncha smokin' babes in the standing room section.

Dave was ogling some babe's cans when her boyfriend saw him checkin' out the goods. He got really steamed and told him to "take a hike." Dave said, "Hey, free country. If your gal doesn't want me peepin' on her hogs, then she shouldn't have 'em on display." Wrong answer.

The chick punched his balls and called him a pervert. That's when security escorted him out. If there's one thing that'll get you kicked out of a baseball game, it's grabbing your sore swollen groin while a babe calls you a pervert.

SUNDAY, AUGUST 21, 2011

Dave's still complainin' that his balls are all swollen. Keeps puttin' ice in his pants. I'm goin' anywhere but here for the rest of the day.

MONDAY, AUGUST 22, 2011

Got home early today. Caught Dave eating Miracle Whip with a spoon out of the jar. Worried that this has been going on for a while. Anyone who eats Miracle Whip out of the jar must have some demons. Sure, I'll eat a spoonful of blue cheese dressing from time to time. So decadent. But I do it in moderation. I'm not some maniac. Plus, it's technically a cheese product. And cheese stands alone.

13

BRENDA AND CONDOLENCES TO DAVID

AUGUST 25-SEPTEMBER 26, 2011

THURSDAY, AUGUST 25, 2011

Really lookin' forward to the weekend, you guys.

Dave ran into my old flame from high school, Brenda, at Paddy's last night. She had the biggest boobs in class. Real choice. Brenda said she's havin' a big bash on Saturday and wants us to stop by. If Ann only knew, she'd freak! Can't wait to catch up on old times. Dave said Brenda's not quite as good in the face area anymore, but her cans are still healthy. Maybe even bigger. Whoa.

Did 15 push-ups in the john. Gotta look good for Brenda. Show her I still got the goods. My bod is feelin' tight. Gonna really knock Brenda's socks off. Gotta keep it healthy 'til Saturday. Not gonna eat anything but canned tuna and granola bars 'til Brenda's bash. Wanna get lean and mean in case I take my shirt off. It can happen at any time.

Might hit GNC later. See if there's a supplement that turns fat into poop. It has to exist by now. If I can crap out a few extra lbs. of fat by Saturday, might have to pull the ol' "accidental BBQ sauce spill" and pop my jersey. It's THE move. Anytime you want to take your shirt off in front of a gal, just spill BBQ sauce on yourself. Makes it so you're not showin' off.

FRIDAY, AUGUST 26, 2011

Leaked a little loose stool in my sleep from my diet supplements last night. Turnin' fat into poop isn't perfected yet, I guess.

SATURDAY, AUGUST 27, 2011

Had the runs all day yesterday. At least today's more like the trots. Headin' to Brenda's in a bit. Hope my rear end behaves. I musta pooped out like 7 lbs. of fat in the last two days. Feelin' slim! When you're meetin' up with an old flame, you gotta be at your best.

SUNDAY, AUGUST 28, 2011

Had a blast at Brenda's last night. She threw a monster bash. Musta been 25 people there. It was dynamite.

Dave behaved himself for the most part. I was proud of him. He only ripped one juicy cut (had a ton of brats, understandable) but otherwise kept it together.

I was gettin' righteous on the dance floor. Broke out the funky worm to some Gap Band. Always a crowd-pleaser. Leaked a little stool though. Had to go in the john to ditch my undies due to my funky worm wet gas release. Felt good to go cowboy like a rock star. I worked up a mean sweat with my moves. Asked Brenda if she'd help take off my new Big Dogs tee in private. She obliged with kindness. Offered me a towel.

Brenda took me in her room for privacy so I could wipe my body down. I could tell she liked what she saw. I've been crappin' out fat all week. Brenda's cans looked so delish, I had to get it on. I put some *Back in Black* on her boombox and went in for a little smooch.

Brenda started goin' wild. She took her shirt off and it was ripe bomb city. Big gutso and her face was old, but it was dark and I was randy. When you're gettin' busy with an old flame, it doesn't matter if you're attracted to 'em, you just let the memories heat up the situation.

Brenda undid her bra and the twins fell out like I died and went to hog heaven, you guys. We were gettin' pretty hot and heavy, and I was all over those big beauties. It's been a while. Then Dave busted in to take a crap. Brenda freaked. Dave stood there starin' at Brenda's rack like he's never seen a girl before askin' if he could #2 in her toilet 'cause the other one was occupied.

Thing is, when a man has to make a BM, you let him, even if you're enjoyin' a babe's large-and-lovelies. Brenda's breath smelled like D'reets anyway.

Brenda was kind of a cold fish after Dave saw her cans and destroyed her john while we waited on her bed, but maybe we'll meet up another time. Old flames die hard.

Dave feels bad 'bout ruinin' my second base action. Treated me to some Gardetto's and Vodka-and-Vernors tonight. Real bold combo. Gardetto's has the bold Euro taste that sophisticated snack connoisseurs like myself crave. Almost as good as Combos.

MONDAY, AUGUST 29, 2011

Woke up late today and didn't have time to shower. Gardetto's garlic sweat was pourin' out of my body. My pits were so rank. Keepin' my arms clasped down all day was hurtin' my back so I decided to do a sink scrub in the john. Thought I locked the door but forgot. Vernon came in when I was goin' at my crotch. Last thing I need is everyone to think I'm the hobo guy who washes his balls and pits in the sink at work. Hope Vernon keeps it hush. At the end of the day, what's worse: Havin' a smelly Gardetto's crotch? Or gettin' caught scrubbin' your business in the work sink? I think the answer's pretty obvious, you guys. 'Course, now my crotch is all sore from scrubbin' it with recycled paper towels. No one can say I'm not doin' my part for Mother Earth.

Thinkin' about writin' a letter to *Penthouse Forum* about my hot times with Brenda this weekend. Probably leave out the Dave diarrhea part though. Always wanted to be in *Penthouse Forum*. It's an exclusive club. But it's hard when you're married with only stories about passive hate.

TUESDAY, AUGUST 30, 2011

Just finished up my letter to *Penthouse Forum*. Think it's soundin' pretty good. Not too raunchy, just a little something for the imagination. Tried to keep it as accurate as possible. No need to make up stories just to show off.

Dear Penthouse Forum,

I know this will sound unbelievable, and I don't think I'd believe it either if I wasn't writing it.

A few ticks back, I was groovin' heavy with this dream babe named Brenda. (This was before I got married and all that crap.) Brenda had the some of biggest gazongas in class, and we were hot 'n' heavy. Time went by and we went our separate ways. But when things cooled off with my old lady, I was left high and dry for action. But then my man Dave ran into Brenda at the bar and said her cans were still lookin' righteous. Brenda asked what I was up to and said we should rendezvous at a bash she was throwing. Brats, cold ones, top-shelf margs, the works. Of course I was game and we headed over the next day. The party was in full gear, but I got all nasty from doing "The Worm" on the dance floor. Guess it got Brenda hot and bothered and she asked me back to her private room for a little

show-and-tell. She went to work on my body immediately, taking
my shirt off and my jimjammer got ready to rock. That's when
Brenda's slammin' chest beefers came out and I was goin' wild like
you wouldn't believe. They were hot and juicy with all the fixins. I
went in for the big grab on her double gulps, and she was insane
with carnal desires. Unfortunately, that's when Dave busted in and
interrupted the XXX action, so we never went all the way. I'm sure
I'll see Brenda again some day, but until then, I'm just gonna have to
keep warm at night with the memory of Brenda's breastos supreme.
Keep it rockin', Penthouse, and I will too.

—*Captain Karl*

Dave said that the *Penthouse Forum* letters are made up. Idiot.
Like you can just make up that erotic stuff if you didn't do it.

WEDNESDAY, AUGUST 31, 2011

Happy Wing Wednesday, you guys. Had nine Caribbean Jerks and
nine Blazin'. Took a whizz after and now my sack's on fire. BW3's
should have somethin' on their menu that says, "WARNING: Do not
touch your sack after Blazin' Wings." I'd do a work sink sack scrub-
down, but last time it was a disaster.

Got home tonight and Dave was all spruced up. Said he's goin'
on a date. I hope she REALLY likes Brut cologne. He's actin' all
weird and won't tell me who his date is with. Probably a lie like his
last "date" when I found him passed out in Taco Bell. Dave doesn't
know how to act on a date anyway. You can't just go through an Arby's drive-thru and boink out your peener. Gotta show class. When
I entertain a babe, I do it right: holdin' doors, payin' for steaks, great
convos, and NICE smellin' goods.

If Dave can't tell me who his date's with, I can't tell him he still has the tag on his cargo shorts. Enjoy your night, "St. John's Bay."

Dave never came home last night. Kinda concerned. No way his "date" went well. He probably blew it, got depressed, and crawled in a Dumpster.

Brenda just called to ask if I've heard from Dave today. Weird. Wonder if she set him up with one of her friends and it went bad?

11:45 A.M.

Dave's trashed outside of my work in the parking lot!

12:32 P.M.

Kinda steamed. Dave is out-of-his-mind drunk. He said he went on a date with Brenda and feels really bad about lyin' to me. I guess it didn't go so well. He got all teared up and mumbly like Stan Laurel. Said he couldn't resist Brenda's cans once he got a look and asked her out to Big Boy.

Dave said he only brought $5 and couldn't pay. Brenda got all up in arms about it 'cause she only had a twenty to last her for the week.

Guess Dave pounded a pint of Popov to calm his nerves before the date, so he was a mess. He knew things weren't going well so he went in to grab her "juicy lucys" and Brenda freaked. You can't just go in for a babe's cans in a booth at Big Boy, you guys. Then Dave left Brenda high and dry with the bill but forgot his keys in the booth.

Dave thinks Brenda probably has his Skylark. He went and blew his 5 bucks on malt liquor and walked around all night, not wantin' to face me. I put Dave in the 'Bring to sleep it off. He's a wreck. I feel sorry for him. Hate that he lied to me, but that just means he's insecure. If he just woulda been honest, I woulda told Dave that Brenda would never waste her time on a sack of crap like him and save his feelings. And, let's be honest. Brenda probably just went out with Dave to make me jealous. I'm Captain Friggin' Karl. Bad Boy City, USA. 'Course, I'm not gonna let some haggard old broad from high school come between me and my sack-of-crap buddy Dave. I already had them cans. Dave is my friend. And friends stick together, you guys. First thing after work, we're goin' to get his ride back.

FRIDAY, SEPTEMBER 2, 2011

Went to get Dave's Skylark back from Brenda last night. It was sittin' right out front. She wasn't home so we went in the back door to try and find his keys. Brenda's house is pretty disgusting. Dirty dishes everywhere. Buncha cats. Big framed Patrick Swayze poster though, which was kinda cool.

Dave kept dickin' around instead of trying to find the keys. Went through her fridge for ten minutes tryin' to find his lefties from Big Boy. Then Brenda pulled in the driveway. We had to pile out the back door and hop a fence. Dave pulled his groin and ripped his golf shirt. Not me, I watch *Cops*. Tore over that fence like I stole a Kenwood.

We walked around the block, then I made Dave go up to the door. Brenda wouldn't answer. So rude. Gonna have to break in again later. It was kinda fun, actually. Can see why people do it.

I told Dave he could use the Sebring until we can steal his Skylark back. One rule: No drivin' and strokin'. I know what he does sometimes.

Really lookin' forward to Labor Day weekend. It's the time when we all celebrate our deep hate of our jobs by getting blackout drunk, unless you're an unemployed idiot.

SATURDAY, SEPTEMBER 3, 2011

Gonna take it easy today. Had a big week. Watch some football, sip cold ones, order Papa John's, really gear up for a Sunday/Monday blowout. Gotta be responsible.

SUNDAY, SEPTEMBER 4, 2011

Got pretty messed up last night. Didn't mean to. Tried to take it easy, but the night was callin'. Went to Crazy Cooter's with Dave.

Crazy Cooter is the piece of garbage you hang out with for good times, even though everyone hates his guts. Told Crazy about Brenda takin' Dave's Skylark. He got all nuts about it. Punched a hole in his drywall and made us go over there. Crazy Cooter said he could hot-wire Dave's Skylark. Busted open the window with a cinder block. Said "there was no time for discussion."

Of course, Crazy Cooter had NO IDEA how to hot-wire Dave's car. He just started punchin' the dashboard and screamin' bad words. A bunch of lights came on in the neighborhood and we got the rock outta there. I guess Crazy Cooter is on probation. Might have anger issues. Maybe he just needs a hug? Not from me though. He smells like wet cigarette butts.

MONDAY, SEPTEMBER 5, 2011–LABOR DAY

Haven't really heard about any rockin' parties today. Guess Crazy Cooter drove his motorcycle into his aboveground pool last night and it's a disaster. He said he came home last night all gacked out on his bike, was like, "Fuck it," and gunned it into the side of his pool. Guess he was still steamed after the hot-wire went wrong.

But still, "Fuck it"?! That's your reasoning for slamming a motorcycle into the side of an aboveground pool? Woulda been great to see, I guess. Otherwise, kind of a waste.

Asked Ann what her and the kids are up to. Families are a last-ditch effort for holiday parties, but it'll give her a thrill if I popped by. Ann said she'd rather I didn't, but if I can "act like an adult" I can stop by for "a little." Makin' a booze grab bag and headin' over.

TUESDAY, SEPTEMBER 6, 2011

Had a blast at Ann and the kids' yesterday 'til Tina Carlson started openin' her piehole. Tryin' to butt into my life. Got so steamed.

Tina drinks too much. Just a no-class broad with a catcher's mitt mug. Tryin' to tell me how my earring looks "desperate." She's jealous.

Tina said that I was turning into a real deadbeat, but if I wanted help, everyone's there for me. From her? I'd rather suck a tailpipe.

Her bozo husband Doug said, "Yeah, Karl, we're here for you." Then stuck out his hand for a shake. A real man goes for a pound. Sissy. Put my finger in his chest and said, "Back off, pal." He got my drift. Think anyone ever tries to give Guy Fieri "help" for livin' the rock 'n' roll lifestyle? I don't think so. Anyone who does is just jealous. So I challenged Doug to a shot contest.

Ann saw what was goin' on and tried to stop it. But a shot contest is like a gunfight. Women need to stay out of it. I knocked back five just to take the lead, then told Doug to pick his panties out of his wife's fat keister and step up. Doug said a shot contest was immature. I said, "Your wife's big sloppers aren't. They're well aged."

Burned him down. Tina went all bonkers like some animal. Usin' foul language in front of the kids and everything. Just a no-class bag of garbage. I put all my booze in a bag and told 'em I didn't need to be part of their behavior. I'm better'n that.

On the way out I stopped to whizz on their car. If you can't stand someone's guts, it's ok to take a leak on their car if you really had to go anyway.

WEDNESDAY, SEPTEMBER 7, 2011

Happy Wing Wednesday, you guys. Just ate 24 wings right in Dave's face. Got a dozen lefties too. Not sharing. It's a power move. Sometimes you have to remind the little dog who the big dog is, for no reason at all.

SATURDAY, SEPTEMBER 10, 2011

Just remembered about Dave's Skylark. It's still sittin' outside Brenda's with a busted window. It's been seriously rain-soaked by now. Wet dog city.

When you abandon a car outside of someone else's house, I think you should get a tax write-off. Kids love to play "drivin'." It's like a mini playground.

SUNDAY, SEPTEMBER 11, 2011

9/11. Never forget. Truly a day of patriotism. I'd personally like to raise a toast to all of the fallen Americans. Let's roll, you guys.

If you're not gettin' blackout drunk today for the USA, you should just move your commie butt to Canada. That's what I think. We'll prevail without you.

God bless this goddamn country. I'm so proud of you guys. WE'LL kick the shit out of you if you mess with us. May the eagles soar to the heavens today with the grace of God for the USA forever. Feel like I could drink a thousand beers right now, you guys.

MONDAY, SEPTEMBER 12, 2011

Really draggin' today. Feel like we shoulda had the day off since 9/11 was on a Sunday. Woulda been the right thing to show respect.

TUESDAY, SEPTEMBER 13, 2011

Made a big batch of Bologna Salad Sandwich Spread last night, you guys. Man, sure takes me back. Such a classic. Captain Karl's Olde Tyme Bologna Salad Sandwich Spread is a midwestern treat with savory Michigan flavors the whole family can enjoy.

CAPTAIN KARL'S OLDE TYME BOLOGNA SALAD SANDWICH SPREAD

I like to start with a pound of Koegel's ring bologna. Koegel's is the only way to go in the bold flavor bologna game, you guys. It's been made in the Flint area forever, so you know it's gotta be good. Finely chop the bologna or toss it in your food processor. Dave got drunk and broke ours putting crayons in it, so it was a lot of work to do it by hand, but I managed. Then dice up ½ cup of white onion. Again, if you have a food processor, use it. To be honest, I don't measure the onion—I just guess. Dave lost the measurin' cups at the beach. Idiot. Some people like to use a ½ cup of sweet relish. I like ¼ cup sweet and ¼ cup dill pickles (just a little bold flavor trick). Next we get to the mayo vs. Miracle Whip debate. I like to mix it up and go ¼ cup M-Whip and ¼ cup mayo, but Dave ate all the mayo.

Some people like to add hard-boiled eggs, but I like sticking with straight bologna. No need to screw with Koegel's bologna perfection.

Mix the crap out of it, add pepper and garlic powder to taste or maybe some Lawry's to break it off the chain for bold flavor lovers. I like my Captain Karl's Bologna Spread on Spatz's toast. Picked up a few loaves for the freezer on my last trip to the Bay City Hooters.

Might have Dave tape me makin' my dish to send into Food Network. *Captain Karl's Fine Midwestern Cuisines* would be such a hit, you guys. Dreamin' about my own food show is makin' the day easier. I could never be as big as Guy Fieri but could maybe be #2 on the roster?

I've gotta get outta this job. It's frustrating to be an idea man trapped in a cage when there's so many corncobs out there in the big time. Screw it, I'm leavin' work early. (Family emergency. Wink.) Gonna have Dave tape my Food Network demo. Time to be the shining rock star I know I can be.

WEDNESDAY, SEPTEMBER 14, 2011

Last night's Food Network demo taping was a disaster. Dave kept pointing the camera at my crotch and saying, "What's cookin', Karl?"

Dave doesn't know anything about chasing dreams. He's a real lowlife. Made me so mad I threw my beer at him and he dropped the camera. That camera was vintage. Taped straight to VHS. So convenient. All this digital crap they have now makes it so hard to enjoy your memories right away.

Dave just called. He's been watching my crotchy Food Network demo all day, crackin' up. Wants to send it to *America's Funniest Home Videos.*

If *AFV* shows a video of me makin' Bologna Salad while Dave makes fun of my crotch, I'll make him not be alive anymore. If you've ever been an assclown on *America's Funniest Videos*, you might as well check in your cool card and forget about your life.

Dave said he hid my Bologna Salad crotch video 'cause he thinks he could win *AFV* with it. Won't give it back unless I come up with some "bread." Who calls money "bread"? Who does Dave think he is? Some brother on *Good Times*?

THURSDAY, SEPTEMBER 15, 2011

Really lookin' forward to the weekend, you guys.

Since Dave won't give up the tape of me makin' Bologna Salad while he makes fun of my crotch, I had to get even. I'm a fan of street justice.

Put all the TP, TV remotes, ranch dressing, *Penthouses*, Pizza Rolls, Toaster Strudels, and booze in my trunk. Dave should crack any minute now. When you mess with the bull, you get the horns, right in your keister. Think Steven Seagal said somethin' like that in *Out for Justice*. If a pal is tryin' to humiliate you, you need to ruin their life for a few days, you guys. Healthy competition is what friendship is all about.

Plus, I'm sendin' a beefy male stripper to freak out Dave tonight. Such a classic gag! Might hit up Chili's for some top-shelf margs to celebrate.

FRIDAY, SEPTEMBER 16, 2011

Haven't seen Dave since I left for Chili's last night. Think he might be steamed 'cause I sent him that stripper and stole everything he had to live for. Hope Dave's not dead. I'd be sad for almost the whole weekend. Ha!

SUNDAY, SEPTEMBER 18, 2011

Kinda worried 'bout Dave. Still haven't heard from him. Phone goes straight to voicemail. And he missed the Lions game. They rocked! Hope he's not in a ditch or somethin'. Watchin' the Lions together is kinda a tradition for me and Dave. He never misses it. Except for that one time he had a kidney stone.

I hope the beefy stripper I sent didn't murder him. Never know what offensive crap Dave mighta said with a huge johnson in his face.

I'm gonna make some "Missing Dave" flyers to put up around the neighborhood. Least I could do for a pal. Need a snooze first though. Kinda bombed.

MONDAY, SEPTEMBER 19, 2011

Dave just called askin' if he got any mail. He never gets ANY mail. Then said his dad died so he wouldn't be back until tomorrow.

Really steamed at Dave. Thought we were like family. Didn't know his dad was still alive, but still. It'd be nice to stay in the loop. Plus, Dave's dead dad coulda got me outta work today. And all those tasty down-home potluck funeral eats? Man, feel like I'm missing out. And you KNOW there's gonna be Taco Salad with D'reets at the funeral reception. It's a guarantee. Such a classic. Bold funeral flavors.

Hmm, work doesn't know what day Dave's dad's funeral is. Might tell 'em it's tomorrow. Take the day off to mourn with Dave. Do it up right. When a pal has a death in the family, it's important to show respect and milk it for all it's worth. Turn a negative into a positive.

Really regretting the fake doo-doo stain I put on Dave's sheets. No time to clean it. Maybe he'll be too dead-dad sad to notice.

Writing an email to Nosey Lady to send in the morning about why I won't be in so it's all ready to go.

Dear _____,

   *Sadly, I will not be able to attend work today. Got some
real bad news this morning. I'd call, but I'm a little shaken and
don't want you to hear me get choked up on the phone as I take
pride in my rugged exterior. My close pal David's father passed
away.*

   *Rest assured, I'll be spending the day with David, tending to
his needs during this emotional time. Steaks, hamburgs, cold ones,
the works. Sadness is sometimes cured through the stomach, and
a death isn't just for mourning, it's for celebrating. Dave's dad
wanted it this way. I fondly remember a fishing trip where he said,
"Karl, when I die, make sure you and Dave have a blast for me
'cause I'll be dead. Ain't no good times where I'm goin'." I plan to
keep that promise I made to David's father. I hate to miss work,
but it's the right thing to do in such a moment of tragedy. And
David's dad was in a war, so this is a celebration of our God and
Country as well.*

   *I'll be sure to pass on all you guys' condolences. David
sure could use 'em right now. Also, I might be in a little late on
Wednesday as David's favorite meal is wings and that's his favorite
on Hump Day. It'd be my honor to treat him to a dozen or so if he
feels up to it. Always good to put a smile on a pal's face when he's
feeling in the dumps.*

   *Thanks for all your support in our hour of grief. On behalf of
David, myself, and David's dead father, blessings to you.*

Sincerely,
Karl Welzein

Dave's not home yet. He's "dealing with family death stuff." A time frame would be nice. I made a huge Taco Salad that's gettin' soggy. I'm gonna start the mourning without Dave, I guess. Makin' a pitcher of Mai Tais. Dave's dead dad would appreciate the island flavors. Also, I'm marinatin' some steaks in my special "Remembrance Recipe." Never met Dave's dead dad, but you'll never forget the taste of these rib eyes.

3:35 P.M.
Crap, forgot to send my email to work! They'll understand if it's late. Partyin' hard for a pal's dead dad makes you forgetful.

Gonna crank up some jams. Whether you're gettin' day drunk 'cause some old man died or partyin' your butt off on a Friday night, Bob Seger is always the right choice.

5:38 P.M.
Wish Dave would hurry up and get here. On my third pitcher of Mai Tais and ate all the Taco Salad. Steaks are marinaded to perfection though.

7:40 P.M.
So ripped off these Mai Tais. Wish Dave could see how hard I'm party-mourning for his dead dad. Gonna fire up the grill. Such a great day.

When someone has a family member die, if you don't go bonkers with the drinks and eats, you might as well just spit on their grave, you guys.

WEDNESDAY, SEPTEMBER 21, 2011

The pad was a disaster when Dave came home. Told him about the one-man bash I had for his dead dad. He just went in his room, slammed the door, and went to sleep. Wow. Some "thanks."

I tried to wake up Dave for a very special Wing Wednesday Dead Dad lunch. Wouldn't budge. Went alone and mourned for both of us like a pal. I think Dave is running away from his feelings. Why else would you turn down a FREE Buffalo Wing lunch?! Death does strange things to a man. I mourned so hard at lunch today. Took down 18 wings and 4 cold ones. Feels good to put out positive vibes in a time of grief.

Nosey Lady's up in my business about the "funeral" I had to go to. Wants to see an obit. Don't know the man's name so I can't find it. She's so disrespectful to pry.

FRIDAY, SEPTEMBER 23, 2011

Cold ones, I've had a few.
But then again, had snacks for munchin'.
I did what I had to do, did some Wing Wednesday lunchin'.
Dave's dad died, of course, he's on heaven's highway.
And more, much more than this, it's finally Friiiiiidaaaaaaay!!!!

That was a parody of "My Way" by the #1 Chairman Goombah, Mr. Frankie S. Might send it to Weird Al! Frankie Sinats was one of the greats. Booze, babes, treatin' people like garbage. Just the best. Such a strong Italian hero.

Workin' on the "My Way" parody and thinkin' about Frank got me hankerin' for some Olive Garden. Gonna "whack" some all-you-can-eat breadsticks. Ha!

Might give Ann a jingle. See if she wants a little romance. Olive Garden *was* always our "special place." Drives any babe wild, really.

Hair might be long enough in the back now for a mini rockin' ponytail. If you have a ponytail, you have a ponytail. Size doesn't matter. It's not like your peener. All babes crave a man with any rockin' pony. And Olive Garden.

Olive Garden really stays true to its rich Italian heritage of bold flavors, strong drinks, and healthy chest beefers on the waitresses. A lot of people are turned off by Italians 'cause they're always loudmouth idiots or murderers on TV. But at the Olive Garden, you're family.

Holy crap, Ann is in for Olive Garden! Gonna sneak outta work early. Gotta shower, do some push-ups, put on smellin' goods, and work on my ponytail.

SATURDAY, SEPTEMBER 24, 2011

Olive Garden supper with Ann was a disaster. She didn't notice my rockin' mini ponytail. That was the whole point of the date. So bummed.

I kept turning my back to her like I was checkin' somethin' out, showcasin' the pony. She just asked, "Is there something wrong?"

I told Ann my back was wrenched from an extreme workout sesh and I needed a really deep rubdown. She didn't take the hint.

I knew it was time to get bad to the bone, so I ordered Never Ending Pasta Bowl #5. It was a real power move. If a babe isn't impressed with you eating five bowls of pasta from Olive Garden, she must be havin' lady time and not be interested in romance.

SUNDAY, SEPTEMBER 25, 2011

Feel like I could drink a thousand beers right now. The Lions game is really stressful. Watchin' them play well is like watchin' a slow kid win the Special Olympics. Feels good, but you know they might start a fire later. Sometimes I wish my son was an athletic retarded kid instead of a sissy who only likes magic and Lunchables. Think we'd be closer, like in a movie about a dad with a son who's athletic but retarded.

No-hassle football and excessive drinking on a Sunday is what being separated from your wife and family is all about. I'm livin' the dream.

Wonder if Ann misses my alpha male presence on football Sundays? Pure testosterone in the air, screaming, punching. Real bad boy action.

Dave instigated a house rule of open-door #2s during football so we don't miss anything. I'm so torn on this one, you guys. I can't crap with the door open when Dave's home. He has no problem. Tried all night. Feel like he's got something on me now. So steamed.

MONDAY, SEPTEMBER 26, 2011

Just heard the inventor of D'reets died. First Dave's dad died, now this? All this death is really getting to me. Feel surrounded by it. Gonna make a trunk liquor drink. Maybe have a chat with the Big Man upstairs.

Prayer isn't somethin' you have to do in church. You can pray while stinkin' up the john or drinkin' in a parked car. God is everywhere if he exists. If everyone spent their time on the toilet prayin' for others, the world could be a better place.

I feel like God is a 50/50 shot. But if you only pray when you're on the can, it's not like you wasted any time doin' better stuff when you might just be wastin' your time.

14

ENTER JODY, EXIT ACTIVIA

SEPTEMBER 27-30, 2011

TUESDAY, SEPTEMBER 27, 2011

I was really thinkin' about it this mornin', and I'd have to say that my favorite food is anything that's "piled high to perfection."

A new single mom moved in to our building yesterday. She's got a little boy who had on a Detroit Lions jersey. Might have to make a connection. Always wanted a son who wasn't like mine. Kinda like the big brother program but without all the paperwork. Might have to make up one of my special dishes to bring over as a welcome tonight. Single moms are always hard up for eats. Give a single mom a hot meal, play some catch with her kid, don't smack her around like her ol' man used to, and she's all yours, you guys.

When I show up at Single Mom's door with double cologne, pony rockin', earring, a hot dish like my Captain Carlos's Enchiladas Especial and Van Halen's "Everybody Wants Some" blaring out of our pad to let her know I'm the neighborhood bad boy hero, new mom is gonna lose her mind with carnal desires. I gotta play it cool though. Take it slow and easy.

New single mom's name is Jody. Really dig the sound of it. Kind of a rugged, sexy vibe. Jody smokes INSIDE of her apartment. I can tell she likes to party. She's real laid-back. I quit again a while ago, but had six or seven more menthols with her to be polite.

Brought Jody my Captain Carlos's Enchiladas Especial. Muy authentico bold Mexicali flavors. Loaded with beef and six cheeses, it's always a hit. When I showed up at her door, Jody seemed a little hesitant, but I think my 'rang, pony, and 'logne just screamed, "Well howdy, stranger." When you bring free food and a sixer of importeds to a single mom's door, you could have a bloody axe in your hand and she'd still let you in.

Let me tell ya folks, Jody's son Jesse can really put away the grub for an eight-year-old. He's husky healthy. I call him "Big J." Big J likes Captain Carlos's Enchiladas Especial loaded with sour cream AND ranch. Always nice to see a young man who craves bold flavors. I feel like we really bonded. We both like the Lions AND extra sour cream. He's like the son I wish I had instead of my own.

Jody doesn't say much. She's just happy to watch her *Housewives* programs and smoke. Such a great gal. Really low-maintenance. I gave her the extra long hug before I left. Pulled her in real safe and tight. No smooch. Gotta play it cool, you guys.

Don't know what's up for later. Might stop by Jody's. See what's goin' on.

11:55 P.M.

so bummed an cofused right now. jodys jut might not be ready for a relationsniop". just tyrin to firgure it out over some crown and booz, our gusy.

when a a babes in a rough spt makin an livin like trash, ouo gotta makin it happaen just becaause loves so rare liek a bold flavro.

by you guys, gonnna make barf . . .

THURSDAY, SEPTEMBER 29, 2011

10:35 A.M.

Just woke up in the bathtub to the sound of Dave makin' a massive BM next to me. Really late for work. Wanna die. Could use some OJ.

10:55 A.M.

Called work. Told 'em I was havin' some plumbing issues. By the sound of Dave's BM, it'll probably be true in a few minutes.

When you wake up in a bathtub covered in Funyuns vomit, next to a man whose rectum is exploding, it's time to pull the reins in, you guys.

12:23 P.M.

Fell asleep on the couch! Gonna pound a Rock & Rye and get to work. Really gotta blow up the "plumbing problem" to epic proportions.

6:42 P.M.

I was really draggin' today, so I swiped one of Nosey Lady's Activias from the fridge. Activia is made for gals to lose their chunky dumpers and make their lady parts healthy, but I dig the taste, it's real refreshin'. I'm a modern man. And I figured it'd be a good time to go on a health kick. Really tone up this time. It was perty tasty, so I went for another one. Double health. Then I figured I'd just take down the whole dozen or so she had in there to make it less obvious. When someone steals your car stereo, you know exactly what happened, but when someone steals your whole car, it's just confusing for a while. It's an old hustler's trick from the streets.

My stomach kinda started to hurt. Figured Activia must have some sorta weird lady hormones in it. I started to worry that I'd grow man sloppers, so I went in the john to check out my pecs. Everything still seemed right on time in the chest department though. I guess I shouldn't have had over a dozen in a sitting though. It's too much health. Ten might be the limit? There were some weird things happenin' inside my body. Doubled over in pain. Felt like I was gonna die and really wanted to go to the hospital.

I musta passed out from the pain 'cause the next thing I knew I was wakin' up on the floor of the john and had to hit the can like never before. I could tell by his Rockports that my boy Ken was usin' the stall. I could barely stand up, but I mustered the strength, dropped my Dockers to the ground, and projectile released my #2 into the urinal. Thanks a lot, Activia. You made a grown man's bowels explode into a urinal like a homeless guy in a mailbox. Congratulations.

I got wet doo-doo backsplash all over the rear end of my khakis. Had to sit down for the rest of the day. So embarrassing. Was really sick of this. I wanted to cry, but I'm too macho and my nature won't let the waterworks start. It's in the genetics of an alpha male.

My doo-doo stains had me worried that I might smell like dog crap on a sneaker, so I chewed a whole pack of Big Red to cover up the smell. That Big Red freshness isn't just for good smellin' during a steamy make-out sesh, you guys. Maybe they should advertise their product for multiple uses. "Big Red: It covers up your #2, so next time you're in the john, have yourself a chew." Could be a national restroom sensation.

Activia should really be ashamed of itself. They use Jamie Lee Curtis's smokin' old cans to trick women into buying their product. Activia never shows you their true colors. If every commercial ended with Jamie Lee Curtis gruntin' and groanin' on the pot, wantin' to die from the pain, people might think twice. Activia is evil.

No matter how much Activia old gals eat, their jugs will probably still be sloppers, not primo bombs like Jamie Lee Curtis's. They should say no to Activia.

FRIDAY, SEPTEMBER 30, 2011

Nosey Lady sent out a memo about not eating other people's food this mornin'. First off, she coulda just lost those Activias. She doesn't KNOW anyone took 'em. And secondly, it's not stealin' if you're helpin' someone out. If she knew what I went through, she'd have to thank me. I suffered for her and didn't even want credit, just like Jesus did. Maybe someday, I'll let her know. Really rub it in her face and make her feel guilty, just like the Big Man upstairs.

It's important to look out for others' safety. That's just how humanity works. Decided to write a letter to the FDA letting them know about the dangers of Activia:

To Whom It May Concern at the FDA,

Greetings. My name is Karl Welzein, and I have an urgent message for you about Activia Yogurt.

Yesterday, I was feeling under the weather due to a late night rendezvous with a new squeeze. Her name is Jody, not that it matters, but I just thought I'd let you know so it doesn't sound like I'm faking. I was late for work at my place of employment, and didn't have time to get a quality lunch. Lunch is important to me. Seeking nutrition and health, I borrowed on of my co-worker's Activias from the community fridge. It had a nice flavor, although not as bold as the ones I usually crave. Also, it was a small portion, so I decided it would be best if I just polished off all 12 of them for maximum health benefits. I thought about leaving some for my co-worker as they belonged to her, but to be honest, her body is past the point of no return.

I believe that she was tricked by the Activia advertisements into thinking that if she consumed their product, her old body would be dynamite like Jamie Lee Curtis' as she continues to have a healthy firm chest area despite her age. You catch my drift.

Shortly after I consumed the 12 Activias, my internals began twisting, causing pain as if I was about to give birth. I considered going to the hospital, but a bold flavor man like myself should be able to handle a few lady yogurts. I regularly consume 18 Mango Habs on Wing Wednesday, so you know I'm a rugged macho man who doesn't become ill easily.

Moments later, I awoke from passing out on the floor of the john, ready to release the evil Activia from my distressed bowels. Ken was in the stall, so I was forced to have a projectile movement into the urinal, soiling my trousers. It was embarrassing, especially to a cool customer such as myself.

Therefore, I am urging you with great passion to remove Activia yogurt from all store shelves at once. But please, I want to make clear that this has nothing to do with Jamie Lee Curtis and her ripe mature chest. If she'd like to discuss this issue, I'd be happy to treat her to something bold in my neck of the woods. Just a friendly meet up, but then, who knows? I look forward to your response. Together, let's help keep America safe.

Sincerely,

KARL WELZEIN

Karl Welzein, concerned USA citizen.

15

JODY AND BIG J

OCTOBER 1–19, 2011

SATURDAY, OCTOBER 1, 2011

Wanted to hang with Jody last night. She wasn't home so I decided to just play it cool by her door and hang out. Babes dig bein' caught off guard with surprises. I got a little worried after two to three hours and ran home to get some snacks. Ruffles, cold cuts, 12-pack of Busch, jumbo olives. Full spread. When you're stakin' out a babe's apartment for her safety, it's best to have some quality eats and plenty of cold ones to keep your energy up.

I polished off all the cold ones and snacks and had a few pee breaks with shots of 'Cardi. Guess I passed out in front of Jody's door. She must have come home when I was takin' a snooze. Didn't wake me up. So caring. She's a good woman.

I hadn't rapped at Jody yet today so I stopped by with some of my QB Karl's Touchdown Chili. Jody asked if I'd mind watchin' her son Jesse while she stepped out with her friends, and I was glad to oblige. It's good to see a trust forming. I love hangin' with Big J. For an eight-year-old, he's got a good head on his shoulders. And he had three bowls of my QB Karl's Touchdown Chili like a real man.

We're watchin' the Tigers. Faygo Red Pop for him. Cold ones for myself. Gonna do some Pizza Rolls in a bit (Big J's fav). Love this kid.

Big J had a sip of my cold one. Pumpkin Ale with bold autumn flavors. He LOVED it. Think him and my son got switched at the hospital.

Think I'm just gonna let Big J finish off that Pumpkin Ale. Kids have strange germs. Gotta drink responsibly, you guys.

SUNDAY, OCTOBER 2, 2011

I got pretty bombed with Big J last night and passed out. When I woke, Big J was just drinkin' one of my cold ones and eatin' Pizza Rolls. He's such a good kid.

Jody didn't get back 'til 3 a.m. Had Big J all tucked in, and he only puked once. I think Jody was impressed, but she had to lay down in the john.

Stopped by Jody's to see what's up this afternoon and Jody said she had go run some important errands with her friend. Told her I'd hang with Big J. It's good to show Jody I can provide support.

I made me and Big J a huge platter of Captain Carlos's Macho Nachos for the Lions game. It all starts with a chipotle ranch base. That's my secret. I told Big J he could have an ice-cold Busch for the Lions victory. Someone's gotta show him how to be a man. Age eight is important for development.

MONDAY, OCTOBER 3, 2011

Big J drew me for his art class homework. My suggestion. I helped a lil' with some final touches. I think it rocks! The theme was "heroes."

RockN' PONY

BY [signature]

LIONS!

Spilled a cold one and some pizza sauce on the drawing, but I think it really captures the moment of creativity, you guys. I might have Big J do a few more drawings. Think this kid really has something special. Gotta nurture his talent.

Big J just called on his burner. Guess the teacher wouldn't let him put his drawing up 'cause it was messy. He's so bummed. I told him we'll make a better one. I'm so steamed at Big J's teacher. But like I always say, when life gives you a problem, you kick that son of a bitch in the teeth. This is America, not some pinko garbage country. These colors don't run, you guys.

Think the new drawing for Big J's school came out dynamite. I "helped" a lot more this time. He signed it and did some lettering though.

When you pose for any type of portrait, sunglasses just bring out the cool. I'm always more confident in my Maui Jims, you guys. We had a little "creative control" argument and his picture got torn, but some tape and staples fixed 'er right up. Big J is pretty strong. Almost had me there for a second.

If Big J's art teacher doesn't put his drawing of me, that I worked hard on, up on the wall of heroes, I'm goin' down to that school.

6:45 P.M.
Big J's kinda down. His teacher wouldn't put up his new picture of me on the hero wall. I drew the damn thing myself! Really steamed.

I'm rockin' a pony, a 'rang, smooth Kangol ("KARL"), gold chain, AND a badass Van Halen logo just for decoration. What part of "hero" doesn't this corncob understand?

I'm makin' Big J a batch of my Woppy Karl's Baked Spaghetti. Loaded with spicy Italian sausage, it's off the chain with macho comfort.

I told Big J, whatever doesn't kill you makes you stronger. Unless you get run over by an Oldsmobile and you're crippled for life or some crap.

I'm goin' down to that school at lunch tomorrow. Gonna get up in that teacher's face. Really take him to Maniac City. Gotta bring the thunder.

WEDNESDAY, OCTOBER 5, 2011
Just got back from Big J's school. I stopped for a dozen Mango Hab Wings and several cold ones first. Had to be on point with bold strength.

They wouldn't let me in because I'm not his "parent." I got all up in the security guard's face, bad boy style. He was no Dalton from *Road House*.

Told that security guard that I had important business with Big J's art teacher. He kept asking, "Who's Big J, sir?" Got really steamed. I told him, "Big J's my main man!" Then he asked if I'd been drinking. Yeah, I'm an ADULT. And I had three or four brews with lunch because I can. That's why.

The security guard said he was gonna call the cops. It's such a sissy move. I didn't want a problem so I hit the bricks peacefully. I'm just gonna find that teacher's address and handle it on the streets, in neutral territory.

I'm gonna stay in tonight and focus. Do some push-ups and drink a KFC gravy straight for pure protein. I gotta look jacked when I go muscle Big J's art teacher.

Focus. Power. Dedication. Strength beyond strength. KFC gravy. These are the tools to get a man's job done with a power move.

THURSDAY, OCTOBER 6, 2011

I told Big J to do some recon and go through the art teacher's desk. Gotta get that address. He's gonna crap when he sees me poundin' on his door like a psycho.

I'm takin' down a whole jar of extra chunky Skippy. And been doin' push-ups in the john all day. Really turning my body into a one-man gang, you guys.

Told Dave he could come hang with me and Big J while Jody's out for the night. I don't want him to feel neglected.

FRIDAY, OCTOBER 7, 2011

Tryin' to piece together last night, you guys. Really hurtin' after the Tigers won and we had a little celebration. Looks like we did it right judin' by how destroyed the pad is. Looks like Big J did some of his art pieces on the wall. I'm pretty sure I encouraged it. Looks pretty good, actually. 90% of the kitchen is covered in either barf or smashed Pizza Rolls. It all looks the same, hard to tell the difference.

I told Big J he could have the day off from school. Frankly, I don't want him goin' back there until I kick his art teacher's ass back to 1984.

Had Big J call work as my son. Told him to say, "Daddy took mommy to the *hopsbital*." Love this kid.

SATURDAY, OCTOBER 8, 2011

Might hit up Jody for some one-on-one time. Big J's cool to hang with, but I think it's time to take our relationship to the next level. When it's time to get hot and heavy with a babe, you just know by the feeling you get in your heart and your groin, you guys.

Had Dave trim my neck up for tonight to really give my pony some framework. Idiot took a chunk out of my ear trimmin' my neck hair. HOW AM I SUPPOSED TO SHOWCASE MY 'RANG WITH A BAND-AID OVER IT!?!

SUNDAY, OCTOBER 9, 2011

Kinda bummin' today, you guys. I had a heart-to-heart with Jody last night. Love is like war, and she really sank my battleship.

I told Jody I wanted to take the next step and turn up the heat in the romance department. Really crashed and burned. Jody said we couldn't "make it" 'cause she's kinda been in a long-distance thing with some guy who lives in Canada. At least she was honest. I said I understood and didn't want to be part of a messy love triangle. I just don't have room in my busy life for any complications.

If I wanted to, I'm sure I could've brought out my power moves that Jody couldn't resist. But that's not my style. I'm a gentle lover. When I look deep into a babe's eyes with my move called the "carnal stare," combined with my masculine aroma, they just melt with desire.

Don't know how I'm gonna break the news to Big J that me and his mom are kaput. Might go get a 7-Up Cake from Kroger to soften the blow.

I mean, I can't blame Jody. How am I supposed to compete with a guy from Canada? I'm a bold catch, but he's an international lover.

I'm gonna have Big J over for the Tigers game. Stocked up on goodies. One last hurrah with Big J is the least I could do. He's my main man. Cheddar & Sour Cream Ruffles, Dean's French Onion, Pizza Rolls, Johnsonvilles, plenty of Faygo, Little Debbie Swiss Rolls, Hormel, and Velveeta with my own special bold spices for a Crock Dip, Lit'l Smokies in BBQ, cold ones up the wazoo. The works. Full spread.

Gotta give Big J one last beautiful evening with the alpha male in his life before I rip his heart out at the end of the game with the bad news.

At least the game should really provide a buffer for the pain. Sometimes I think the Tigers are all Big J has that makes him happy.

MONDAY, OCTOBER 10, 2011

The Tigers lost last night so I didn't have the heart to break the bad news to Big J. Maybe tonight. Just so conflicted. Plus, there's a Lions game AND a Tigers game today, and we have the day off for Columbus Day, so I should be toasted by then. Best to be nice and bombed when you break a kid's heart.

TUESDAY, OCTOBER 11, 2011

Really hurtin' today, you guys. Woke up on the kitchen floor. My back's a disaster. Nothin' says you've truly lived life like wakin' up in the morning, feelin' like you're gonna die, you guys.

Took a mean nap in the work john for most of the afternoon. Nothin' like cold tile and white noise flushes to rejuvenate the mind and body. Vernon came in and asked what I was doin' layin' on the john floor. I told him I had a bad back. He said, like Larry Bird? Kinda racist.

Pretty banged up, you guys. The Tigers playoffs are really wreakin' havoc on my body, but it's my duty as a Michigan man to do my part.

Plus, I finally had to break the news to Big J last night. Got pretty bombed and went over to Jody's to wake him up at 2 a.m. Slammed on her door for a half hour before she answered. Kinda rude to make me wait like that. 2 a.m. or not, it's always time for manners. I woke Big J up and told him we couldn't be bros 'cause his mom didn't want to do adult things with me like have erotic passions. I let him know, when a gal doesn't have the carnal desire to fill a man's needs, it's time to move on down the line to New Babe City.

He was confused, so I had to go man-to-man with "We're over Big J, hit the bricks." He looked sad, but I had to whizz so I split. When you break some horrible news to a kid, it's best to do it as a surprise in the middle of the night so it just feels like a nightmare.

Thank God it's Wing Wednesday. Such a great cheer-me-up from destroying the world of a young child. When life is hard, get yourself some wings.

Really lookin' forward to the weekend, you guys.

What a day. Cut out of work early to see my "back doctor." Watched the Tigers go off the chain with my bro Al at Paddy's. Welzein bad boys!

Got a little too smashed on top-shelf margs. But when I'm rollin' with my bro Al, we gotta keep our title as the Bad Boy Party Kings of the Flint area. After the Tigers won, I ripped off my shirt and started Hulkin' up. I was asked to leave. Guess my healthy body is threatening.

I went to wait in the Sebring for Al but couldn't get the door open with my key so I smashed in the window. Guess I was flyin' high with emotions. The good news was, it turned out to be someone else's car. Had to get the rock outta there. Hope they had insurance. When you destroy someone else's property, it's ok to just take off if it was truly an accident, you guys. Especially if you're pretty drunk.

FRIDAY, OCTOBER 14, 2011

I really got into it with Dave last night. He was in one of his moods. Dave said the Tigers had no chance so why was I pumped that they won?

I got really steamed. Told Dave that he had no chance at life so why does he even get his wide load out of bed in the morning?

Then Dave made some crack about my "momma," so I smashed my PB&J-and-Fritos sandwich in his face. Hate to waste food, but he crossed the line. Decided to keep it civil, so I challenged Dave to a body-blow contest. It was time to man up. The contest really escalated quickly. Everything in the pad is pretty much broken.

Lamps, plates, glasses, coffee table, my Blatz sign, the boob tube, the Van Halen carnival mirror, pretty much everything is destroyed. Dave says I have to buy him a new Vizio 'cause I ripped his off the wall tryin' to give him a wedgie. Whatever. They're only like 60 bucks.

Feel so terrible. Made a V8 Bloody out of my trunk liquor. This is an emergency. Goin' to sip it in the john and catch some toilet z's.

7:45 P.M.

Just woke up on the toilet at work. Everyone left. Felt so alone. No one even noticed I was in the john. It kinda hurts. Goin' to Chili's to think about my life.

SATURDAY, OCTOBER 15, 2011

Super pumped for the Tigers game. Sippin' Vodka-and-Vernors, had Dave make a run to Taco Bell in the 'Bring, and the new Vizio is rockin'! Wonder why they don't make cases for TVs like they do for cell phones in case you get in a full-on brawl with your pal over yo momma jokes?

I bet my main man Barry O. is down with the Tigers. A cool soul brother like our prez is definitely a Motown man. I used to be a big fan of George W. He rocked. But when a smooth homeboy from the hood like Barry O. takes over, you just have to get down, you guys. Barry O. showed the country that anybody could be president. Wonder if Deion Sanders has considered running? President Primetime!

Where the crap is Dave? I'm gettin' kinda loaded. Could use that Taco Bell to come mop up the booze. It'd really hit the spot.

3:37 P.M.
Sick of this. And where's my dang Taco Bell?!

5:20 P.M.
Where the hell is Dave? Feel like he's been gone forever. He missed the whole game. I'm pretty ripe. Could sure use that Taco Bell magic.

9:45 P.M.

Worried about Dave. Shouldn't have let him take the 'Bring. It's a smokin' ride. Hope he didn't pick up a gal at Taco Bell or die. Want my XXL Chalupas! Idiot won't pick up his phone. So steamed.

SUNDAY, OCTOBER 16, 2011

Dave didn't come home 'til way after I passed out last night. He was actin' really strange this morning. Put the screws to him for info, but he just kept sayin' stuff like "dunno." Kinda par for the course for Dave, but still, seemed shady.

I went to get something out of the 'Bring (booze) and Dave got all shaky and beet-red. Then he just spilled the beans with that Stan Laurel blubber face of his. I guess he was revvin' the engine in the Taco Bell drive-thru, tryin' to impress some babes, then he moved up in line and forgot the 'Bring was in drive, went to rev again, and smashed into the truck in front of him. There wasn't any damage to the truck, but the trailer hitch went though the 'Bring's front end. Dave said he took it to Crazy Cooter's to get it fixed. Crazy Cooter's brother Squirrel used to work at Auto Zone and said he can do it for like 60 bucks.

So steamed at Dave, you guys. Tigers lost today, Lions lost today, Dave crashed my 'Bring, I never got any Taco Bell. . . . ANYONE ELSE WANT TO CRUSH MY SCROTUM WITH A TIRE IRON?!

MONDAY, OCTOBER 17, 2011

Had to take a cab to work today. Pretty regal. Made sure a few people saw me before I got out. Felt like a rock star. Think I really blew everyone's mind. Makes me look more mysterious.

Took a cab to work again. Takin' a cab to work is so decadent. Made a plate of eggs and toast for the ride. Felt like I shoulda asked somebody for Grey Poupon. Crazy Cooter said Squirrel wanted to get the 'Bring fixed "just right" and needed until the end of the business day. Thought that was cool 'cause you gotta appreciate good old-fashioned elbow grease and dedication. Then I went to pick it up after work.

It's not fixed at all. Really steamed, you guys. Squirrel just painted the damaged bumper with spray paint and put a Harley-Davidson sticker over the busted headlight. Said I owe him $60! Sure, a Harley sticker is classic cool. Shows you're not to be messed with. But it's NOT 60 bucks OR a headlight. At all. Told Squirrel I had to scrape the bread together and pay him later. And "later" = "never." Really P.O.'d.

Sick of this.

Took another cab to work today. It's hard to go back to drivin' myself when life has been so plush. Must be what Donald Trump would feel like if he was cool instead of not cool.

Had to get another cab to go to B-Dubs for Wing Wednesday. Hope some of the waitresses saw and had a "Who is THAT guy?!" moment. Could really pay off later. Lotta smokin' hot babes at B-Dubs I've been eyeballin' since way back.

I really gotta get that headlight fixed on the 'Bring. Gotta big weekend comin' up. Can't risk a DUI. It's important to be responsible and safe, you guys.

I never understood having a "designated driver." Why would anyone ever wanna hang out with someone who'd agree to do that?

16

KAREN AND THE BIG B-DAY CELEBRAISH

OCTOBER 20-24, 2011

THURSDAY, OCTOBER 20, 2011

Really lookin' forward to the weekend, you guys.

Hit it off with a babe last night at Paddy's. I think her name was Karen. Mmmm . . . Ka-ren. Such a sexy name. Really just rolls off the tongue. I gave her a lift home in my private cab. I think she was really impressed 'cause things got pretty hot 'n' heavy with bold cab romance flavors. My problem in the romance department might have been drivin' myself around. Takin' a cab lets you go "hands free," if you catch my drift. Man, when you're frenchin' a babe in the back of a cab and feelin' on some chest beefers over the shirt, you really understand what God is all about. I'm flyin' HIGH after that rendezvous. I-think-her-name-is-Karen might be the best thing that's ever happened to me in a while.

Should even thank Dave for crashin' my 'Bring into that Taco Bell and forcing me into the world of luxurious personal cab drivers.

Gonna head back to Paddy's tonight. See if Karen's hangin'. I got a big birthday comin' up on Sunday. Have to see if she wants to be the icing on my cake. Ha! Man, Karen sure would be some nice arm candy for my big b-day celebraish on Sunday. I'm goin' heavy on the 'logne. Wanna drive her wild. Dave said he always soaks his ball-sack in Brut before a big date. That's probably a reason why Dave never goes on any dates.

Just smoked a little grass to get relaxed for my rendezvous. It's legal so it's cool. Why is it ok to drive on grass and not booze? Crankin' up some Seger to get pumped for Karen, then I'm headin' out. When it comes to babes, rock 'n' roll never forgets, you guys.

FRIDAY, OCTOBER 21, 2011

Friday eyes! (clap clap) They're watchin' you! (clap clap) Friday eyyyyyyyyyes! They're watchin' you watchin' you watchin' you-ou-ou-ou!

I hung out at Paddy's 'til close. No sign of Karen. Got pretty bombed. I finally lost my cool and started yellin' out, "KAREN!!!" Not my proudest moment. I'm really concerned about not hookin' up with her. I've never done it before, but Dave said to try Craigslist Missed Connections. Seems like romance happens there. Hope it works.

HOT RENDEZVOUS WITH KAREN?-M4W (GRAND BLANC)

Looking for a smokin' babe named Karen (I think.) We got pretty bombed on top-shelf margs at Paddy's, then took it back to my private cab for adult carnal desires. I thought your chest beefers were off the chain, and when we frenched it was outta bounds with bold flavors. You've really got the stuff to be my main birthday squeeze on Sunday, when I'll be poundin' cold ones in Bad Boy City, USA. Would love to get down again, maybe in one of my private cabs or at your place? Who knows. We just can't take it back to my pad 'cause Dave is a real corncob and I want it to be just one-on-one when the heat gets turned up. I crave your touch. Let's rock!

Stayed up all night waitin' on word from Karen. Hope she gets back to me soon or I might have to make plans with another babe for the celebraish.

I think Dave might be plannin' somethin' big for my bash. He's been in the john more than usual. Takes all his calls in there like he's Fonzie. I can't wait for tomorrow. It's gonna be slammin', you guys. Besides, if I roll solo, I'll have my choice of any gal. Them's birthday rules. So pumped. I feel like I could drink a thousand beers right now. Gotta take it easy though. Gonna lay low and get my outfit just right.

Dave's keepin' it real hush about my celebraish. He never even said happy b-day to me. I'm tryin' to play it cool. But I rented a Hummer limo to pick up the party crew in about an hour. Make sure we all show up in style. No clue what the plan is. Maybe Chili's first to start it off, then who knows?

I put up another Craigslist message just in case Karen or whatever her name is didn't see the first one. My birthday body is throbbing for her touch, you guys:

APB FOR KAREN!!! CHILI'S AND MAYBE MORE-M4W (GRAND BLANC)

Karen, hope you get this message. It's me, Karl. Just to refresh your memory, I was the smooth fella with the rockin' pony and hoop 'rang that you got all comfy and cozy with in my private cab after Paddy's last week or whenever it was. Time flies when you're having a blast like I am in this crazy world we call "life." Anyway, your kisses went down so smooth. Really moist and consensual. I gotta be honest with ya, babe. I'm just comin' off a crazy situation with a gal named Jody and her son Big J, so you know I'm down for anything involving carnal desires. It's my big b-day celebraish this evening, and I'm perty sure Dave has something off the chain planned. He's keepin' it hush, but I went ahead and got a Hummer limo, just to make sure whatever we do is filled with class and bold automotive flavors. It's so money anytime you show up in a Hummer limo. You don't wanna miss this. Thinkin' about Chili's? Ever been? The service is top-notch and their top-shelf margs really hit the spot. Let's do this. It's tonight. Let me know. Would love to have your body in my arms. And if you want to get hot and heavy in my private HUMMER LIMO afterward, I can boot the party crew out and it'll be hog heaven. Catch my drift? Ha! Sorry, kinda bombed from bein' in Cold One City for the Lions game. Looks like they're really gonna eat it again. Who cares?! Nothing can ruin my celebraish. Oh crap, Dave just tore a ripper. He's been eatin' Pizza Rolls all morning. Me? I'm savin' up my appetite for Chili's and you. Sorry to ramble, but I just can't stop thinkin' 'bout you, babe. Think we could have something special, if only for one night. Be my b-day gal? Hit me up. Let's make it rock into the night! I'm hungry for your touch.

My Lions lost today, but I'm not gonna let it get me down. I smashed a beer bottle in the sink and I'm gonna move on.

Dave's been cold as ice with my b-day bash surprise. I asked him what he was up to later. He said, "Dunno, just hangin' out." When the Hummer limo pulled up outside I told Dave, "There's a Hummer limo parked outside! Check it out!" He didn't even get up. He just said, "Cool," and ripped a juicy wet one.

Dave's been in the john forever. I told him I was going out. He just safety flushed and didn't say anything. I guess the crew must be meetin' me later for a primo surprise.

I'm gonna take the Hummer limo for a spin. Maybe drive by Ann's. Hope she sees me. It'd blow her socks off. Plus, she'll feel so bad when she realizes she forgot about my big day and I didn't need her or the kids at all.

Besides, they've been really slackin' on the b-days for a while. In the old days, it was always streamers, rockin' tunes, tons of eats and drinks, lots of pals, and great gifts like a new Detroit Lions sweatshirt or even a new boombox.

Last year when I was laid up from my heart attack, they gave me a No Doubt CD that my daughters picked out 'cause it was "classic rock" and Ann ordered a veggie pizza. The No Doubt CD wasn't even wrapped.

MONDAY, OCTOBER 24, 2011

Had a rough one last night. Really hurtin', you guys.

I took my Hummer limo to Chili's. Was feelin' top-notch. Figured the crew must have had something planned at my favorite spot. I took down about seven top-shelf margs, then waited to order eats until the gang showed up. I wanted to be polite, not some pig-out slob.

Chili's booted me out when they closed at 10 p.m. I told 'em it was my b-day celebraish and they could suck it. Thanks a lot for the warm wishes, Chili's. I shouldn't have thrown a shot glass at the waiter, but that corncob had no right to toss me out on my b-day. I DON'T CARE IF YOU'RE CLOSED, CHILI'S.

So I took the Hummer limo over to Ann's. Last thing I remember is makin' the driver crank up "Hollywood Nights" on repeat so I could blow her mind. I woke up there in the morning. Guess I had a leaky man faucet 'cause my pants were soggy. I guess Ann might've seen me in the Hummer limo when she took the kids to school in the morning. She probably got jealous of my rock star lifestyle.

On your birthday, it's not IF you wet your pants in your sleep, it's how many times. It's a natural tradition. For the record, I'm guessing three, not to brag or anything.

I had the Hummer limo just take me straight to work. My pee pants were mostly dried so that was cool. And it's not like I BM'd myself. I'm not some hobo, you guys. Nosey Lady saw me pull up to work in the Hummer limo and asked me, "Why?" Her dumb mouth was all hangin' open. She's not used to any sort of class. I told her it was for the celebraish! She just shook her head. Stupid know-nothing sow.

I spent most of the morning sleepin' on the toilet. When your friends and family all forget about your b-day, who cares. But when I got off the john, a miracle happened. My bro Al sent a big box of Omaha Steaks to my work. I really rubbed it in everyone's face. Made 'em all feel terrible for being rude and thoughtless. Omaha Steaks are pretty much the best in the world. So juicy and succulent. And that's what I'm gonna tell Dave when I eat 'em right in front of him.

The best revenge for a pal forgettin' your b-day is eatin' somethin' he can't afford while he has to watch. Really make him feel like some sorta street animal, beggin' for the scraps. Such a power move.

17

McRIBBOWEEN

TUESDAY, OCTOBER 25, 2011

Got some great news today. THE McRIB IS BACK, YOU GUYS!!!

Don't know why Mickey D's ever has to "bring back" the McRib. A bold taste sensation like that shouldn't ever be goin' anywhere. When they decided to take the McRib away again, those Wall Street hippies should do something worthwhile and "occupy" McDonald's headquarters. That whole Occupy Wall Street thing just looks like an excuse to hang out and complain all day. MY USA was built on hard work. If you don't have a job, maybe you should try "occupying" an Arby's restroom with a mop and stop whinin' about bein' broke. Those white hippies just want everything handed to 'em. They don't have any priorities about what's important.

Just noticed Halloween is around the corner. I gotta start plannin' out my costume. Might go as the Red Rocker, Sammy Hagar. Man, he is one cool customer. Gonna go for a drive to Mickey D's to clear my head and plan it out. Gettin' me another McRib. They're for a limited time so I gotta take advantage. Plus, McRibs aren't fried so it's a healthy pork.

WEDNESDAY, OCTOBER 26, 2011

Today at lunch I stopped off for a McRib on the way to BW3's so I kept it light and healthy with a dozen Mango Habs (no fries). Stomach got kinda upset. Felt like the McRib and the Mango Habs were havin' a 1%-er gang war over bold flavor territory. Funny thing 'bout the McRib is you still crave another one while you're hurtin' from the last one. It's kinda like beer and havin' to take a whizz, I guess.

On the way home from work, I stopped off for two more McRibs. Startin' to kinda understand why they're only for a limited time. It's for public safety.

THURSDAY, OCTOBER 27, 2011

Really lookin' forward to the weekend, you guys.

Gotta get goin' on my Halloween costume. Still thinkin' 'bout goin' with Sammy Hagar, but Guy Fieri would just be so money. It's a tough call, both are badass. Dave said he wants to go as Stone Cold Steve Austin. I told him, "More like Cold Stone Steve Creamery." Burned him so hard.

Always loved a rockin' Halloween celebraish. It's when babes let everyone know what their bodies look like. It's kind of a tradition. Plus, when you're at a Halloween celebraish, it's ok to ogle any babe and express your carnal desires with open compliments on their chest beefers.

The more I think about it, the more I'm leanin' toward goin' as Guy Fieri. Sexy, arousing costumes aren't just for the ladies, you guys.

FRIDAY, OCTOBER 28, 2011

Happy Friday to ya, you guys! Only worked a half-day. Had some nasty D this mornin'. Musta got some bad fries with my McRib last night. Might have to alert Mickey D's about their bad fry situaish. I can't be holed up in the john during McRib season. It's for a limited time! Think I feel some more D comin' on. Got another (two) McRib on the way home to take advantage and a SMALL fry. Figured they'd be fresh by now, but I was wrong. That's it. I'm goin' to work on my letter in the john. I don't have time to go "occupy" a business like some scumbag on welfare when I have a problem. But, to be fair, if a company gives you diarrhea, there's no way you can "occupy" anything of theirs without fillin' your pants. It's smart business. Maybe those Wall Street guys should think about how to give people the runs. 'Cause if you've got the runs, there's no way you're sittin' around causin' problems, you guys.

SATURDAY, OCTOBER 29, 2011

Finished up my letter to Mickey D's about their bad fries. Gonna mail it in after grabbin' a quick McRib for lunch.

Dear McDonald's,

Karl Welzein here, hailing from Grand Blanc, MI. Before we get into things, just wanted to let you know that I've always been a fan of your value menu as well as your premium items featuring mayo, tomatoes, and lettuce. They really hit the spot, you guys.

Would like to start off by giving you bold kudos for bringin' back the McRib. It's a bold taste sensation that can't be beat and always leaves me lusting for more. It's like you put some sort of vitamin "Crave" in the pork that makes my mouth water. Unfortunately,

I have to be the bearer of bad tidings. I've been gettin' busy with the bold McRib flavors two to three times a day since you broke it out for the big McRib celebraish. The quality of the sandwich is just top-notch and even though Ken from work told me you use ingredients found in gym mats or some crap, I understand that bold tastes sometimes have to come from exotic locales. Think there was an episode of Bizarre Flavors *where the hefty gay fella eats a giraffe vagina that he said tasted like a BM sandwich but had nutty aromas that reminded him of a trip to the Philippines. Really opened up my mind to new tastes, textures, and sensual culinary cravings only found in places like Europe. So, big ups to you, Mickey D's. If gym mat dust really makes the tastes shine through in the McRib, then I'll go hand-in-hand with you in giving the food squares a "suck it" for being so closed-minded. Now, let's get back to business.*

A few days ago, I started having to spend large portions of my day on the john because of bad fries. Even with the two to three McRibs I take down every day like a real badass, I just can't resist getting your crispy golden fries. Except for KFC gravy, they're perty much the only food you can drink out of a cup. Dave is kinda P.O.'d that I've been hoggin' the john so much with my nasty D, but I told him I'd get in touch with Mickey D's, asap. I must strongly urge you to contact my local franchise and have them check out the fry situaish. I can't be usin' up all the TP 'cause Dave has some personal D issues as well. And TP doesn't grow on trees.

Thanks for your time, you guys.

Sincerely,
Karl Welzein

P.S. Bring back the McDLT!

Crazy Cooter had his big Halloween celebraish last night. Forgot I owed his bro Squirrel 60 bucks. Things got kinda heated. Can't believe Squirrel recognized me in costume. Decided to go as the Bold Bad Boy, Guy Fieri. Had Dave bleach my hair and beard. It burned pretty bad and some patches fell out, but it looked so money. I had the front and back shades too. The works. I really turned it up. Any real man knows you don't dress up in some goofy costume for Halloween. Makes you look like a corncob. You gotta go with somethin' badass: Dalton from *Road House*, Steven Seagal, Renegade from *Renegade*, Guy Fieri . . . all badass 'stumes that make the ladies crave your touch.

Squirrel was screamin' that I owed him "60 bones" and said to "cough up the bread." Like I was gonna give in to a guy in a hot dog costume. I told Squirrel he could kiss my bold-flavored butt if he thought he was ever gonna see the 60 bucks for his hack automotive work. I was so steamed.

Squirrel grabbed a fork and said he was gonna "get gnarly" on me if I didn't pay. Dave hit the bricks like a sissy, dressed like Stone Cold. Idiot. If you wear a Stone Cold Steve Austin 'stume for Halloween and flip out when some maniac gets a little stabby with a fork, you don't deserve a peener.

I told Squirrel he didn't want a piece of the Bold Bad Boy. He got confused like he didn't know what I was talkin' about, so I showed him.

I picked up a bowl of nacho dip and threw it in Squirrel's face. He started screamin' and ran out in the yard. Guess it was still pretty hot. Decided I should probably split. When you burn a man's face with nacho dip while he's wearing a hot dog costume, it's best to leave the party before more violence happens.

MONDAY, OCTOBER 31, 2011

Really gettin' a lot of attention at work for my new bleached Guy Fieri 'do. Everyone seems pretty jealous. My scalp is peelin', but it's a small price for great style.

Ann called today. Guess my daughters don't wanna trick-or-treat with my son 'cause he's a wuss. Now I have to take him. Great. Kids ruin Halloween. What if I had plans? Ann's so thoughtless sometimes. I'm at least gonna try to show my son what Halloween is all about: disturbing terror and checkin' out babes' cans. It's about time he manned up. Maybe we can bond?

TUESDAY, NOVEMBER 1, 2011

Trick-or-treating with my son was a disaster. I'm sorry, but that guy just sucks sometimes. He dressed up as Harry Potter. Again. I told him his costume should be a role model or hero, like Rambo, not some pretend magician who likes to ride broomsticks.

And every time I'd get groovin' on a babe at a house, my son would freak out at some scary decoration and run away. I wanted to murder him. You don't just bail out when another man's got an opportunity for a late-night rendezvous. He's really got a thing or two to learn about guy code.

I was drinkin' cold ones outta my "adult treat bag" and had to whizz real bad. Told my son to be on lookout while I took a leak on the side of someone's house. He started yellin', "Daddy's makin' pee-pee!" Just kept yellin' it over and over: "Pee-pee! Pee-pee!" I had to stuff my plumbing back in my pants and try to pinch it. It was a disaster. Soaked my Wranglers real bad. I told my son that was it. He ruined both our nights, and I took him home. Ann probably "accidentally" overbought on the candy anyway.

Trick-or-treating is just begging. It should be left to the poor kids who come over from the bad neighborhoods, packed in tuna boats. I did the right thing takin' him home and leavin' candy for the less fortunate. The holidays are all about sharing and charity, you guys.

WEDNESDAY, NOVEMBER 2, 2011

Woke up in a panic this mornin'. Realized I hadn't had a McRib in a few days. They're only for a limited time. You gotta take advantage.

Had a great idea when I was takin' down my third McRib at lunch: If Mickey D's can make a boneless rib sandwich, why not make a boneless chicken wing sandwich shaped like six wings? The McWing could really sweep the nation. Maybe even have it for MORE than a limited time. Spent most of the afternoon workin' on plans for it in my car.

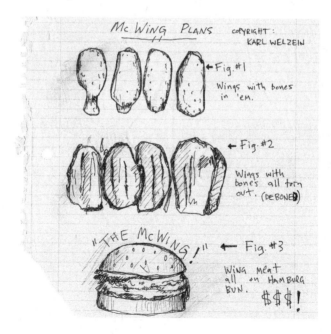

Really lookin' forward to the weekend, you guys. Stayed up 'til 3 a.m. writin' my pitch to Mickey D's for the McWing. Gotta try and set up a meeting. Think it could be winner, winner, chicken dinner.

$ THE McWING $

PLEASURE IS ALL YOURS TO SEE ME TODAY, MICKEY D'S. NAME'S CHEF KARL. AND I'M GONNA ROCK YOUR SOCKS OFF WITH THE TRUE BOLD FLAVORS OF THE McWING. SURE, YOU HAD SUCCESS WITH THE McRIB IN THE PAST. PERTY TASTY. BUT THATS OLD NEWS, GRANDPA McD. WITH THE BOLD GENERATION KICKIN' DOWN THE DOOR FOR INNOVATION, THE TIME IS NOW FOR THE NEW McWING. (stare carnally at some babe in the room and wink, put out the vibe that you're all man. Maybe flex a 'cep?) THE McWING SANDWICH IS 6 DE-BONED WINGS, HYPER FUSED TOGETHER TO MAKE A PATTY LIKE NO OTHER, WITH COATING INSIDE, (DO A SPIN MOVE), AND OUT! PILED HIGH ON WHATEV BUN YOU USE FOR THE McRIB, WITH LETTUCE, TOMATES, GARLIC MAYO, AND CAPTAIN KARL'S KRAZY WING SAUCE, YOU'LL SELL A CRAPLOAD BEFORE YOU EVEN OUT A SIGN UP. ARE YOU STUPID IDIOTS? YOU DON'T LOOK STUPID, EXCEPT FOR HIM→(POINT AT SOME DOLT FOR HUMOR, Everyone cracks up 'cause he just got burned! Ha!) Look, here's a DRAWING I MADE MYSELF. (SHOW BADASS OFFICIAL DRAWING.) You WANT IT. You KNOW IT. (WINK AT THE BABE AGAIN)

THE McWING IS ALL YOURS, FOR A COOL MILLION $. THIS OFFER IS FOR A LIMITED TIME, YOU GUYS. (turn, showcase rockin' pony, walk out, slam door HARD, wait for phone call.)

A true bold taste sensation. Pretty steamed at how EVERYTHING claims to have bold flavors now. Bold flavors are for the country's elite connoisseurs, not just any corncob. The McWing sandwich'll take back bold flavors for the proud Americans who know what it's like to be a Bold Bad Boy, not just some tagalong.

If I can set up a meeting, man, I'll wow 'em with my alpha charm. When you want money from a corporation, you have to really get in their face with an idea and dominate, you can't just camp out on their lawn like a slob, lookin' for a handout. And I'm no stranger to bein' a tough customer. Those pink panty suits at Mickey D's will be beggin' to pay when I hit 'em with my McWing aggression. My speech turned out so money.

Really ridin' high on my McWing idea. Can't wait to get out of work. Feel like I could drink a thousand beers right now, you guys.

FRIDAY, NOVEMBER 4, 2011

Feel like I drank about a thousand beers last night. Made a bunch of McWing prototypes. Some tasty. Some not so tasty. Inventing is a process that takes patience and hard work.

I got a bunch of extra McRibs today. I'm tryin' to find that special secret for the McWing. I think it might be "love." And love isn't an ingredient you can just buy at the store. Gonna go eat a McRib on the toilet, then take a nap. I heard that most geniuses do their best work in the john where there's no distractions. It's just you, the bowl, and your thoughts.

18

HOLIDAYS AND THE HEAD HONCHO

NOVEMBER 11–DECEMBER 26, 2011

FRIDAY, NOVEMBER 11, 2011

Just heard about that Penn State fella. What a corncob. When you hit the showers, just get your body clean and get out. There's no need for horseplay.

SATURDAY, NOVEMBER 12, 2011

Just polished off a KFC Cheesy Bacon Bowl. Move over, McRib, there's a bold new sheriff in Flavor Town.

5:30 P.M.

Bombed on cold ones from watching MSU stomp Iowa. Headin' back to KFC for another CBB. It's ok to drive drunk if it's for food.

SUNDAY, NOVEMBER 13, 2011

Polished off another KFC Cheesy Bacon Bowl. I just can't say enough good things about it. It's a complete hearty meal in itself, you guys.

The KFC Cheesy Bacon Bowl is for a limited time. Gotta take advantage. When KFC adds bacon into the mix, they're pretty much unstoppable. If you don't get a KFC Cheesy Bacon Bowl before they're gone, you're pretty much the stupidest a-hole in town. That's just a fact, you guys. The only way KFC could sell even more Cheesy Double Bs is if the colonel himself shoved a gun in vegan corncobs' faces and made 'em eat it.

KFC really got me thinkin. Seems like "bowls" are all the rage. Think Captain Karl's Pizza Bowls could really sweep the nation.

It could be huge. "Captain Karl's Pizza Bowls are a bowl of bold pizza chunks you eat in a bowl. Only at Captain Karl's Pizza Ship."

THURSDAY, NOVEMBER 17, 2011

Really lookin' forward to the weekend, you guys.

Why don't they make 10-hour Energy? Who only works for five hours and can't make it through their shift at Wendy's? And that sissy in the 5-hour Energy commersh is such a corncob. "I'm so sleepy! Need my coffee!" What he really needs is a morning ass-kicking.

Took down three 5-hour Energies. 15-hour Energy! They should make that. Keeps you rockin' into the night! Gonna go do some push-ups in the john.

5:30 P.M.

Drank another 5-hour Energy. Really crankin'. Headin' to Paddy's, then who knows? Pretty cold out but puttin' the top down. Ready to ROCK OUT ALL NIGHT LONG, YOU GUYS!!!!!!!!!!!!!!!!

3:35 A.M.

Can't sleep. Shouldn't have had 20 hours of Energy. Might toss back a couple cold ones. It's the natural way to hit the sack.

Ann used to take Ambien. She'd turn into a nutso idiot. Except for the one time she thought I was Magnum, P.I. Only time we made it in 2007.

4:47 A.M.
Super bombed. Still can't sleep. Gonna do some shots of Crown. Gotta get some shut-eye, you guys.

FRIDAY, NOVEMBER 18, 2011

Pretty shaken up. Dozed off on the way to work. Woke up drivin' into oncoming traffic. The Big Man upstairs really saved me on this one.

Only got an hour of sleep. Think I might be still drunk but who knows? Everything seems like pretend. Could really use a hug, you guys. Going to catch some zzz's on the toilet. Feel like my heart's gonna explode. Hard to breathe.

SATURDAY, NOVEMBER 19, 2011

I don't know where the 'Bring is. Don't know why I don't have on underpants. Tryin' to piece it together. Thinkin' Arby's was involved.

Car might be at Paddy's? Remember havin' 5-hour Energy Vodka Shots 'cause I wrote down "5hr energy vdka blasts" on my arm.

Out. Musta taken a cab to Arby's. Kinda remember gettin' in a fight with the cab driver 'cause they were closed. Figured we could wait it out. When you're blacked out, you're probably thinkin' Arby's.

Now I remember where my unders are. Oh God. Not good, you guys. Guess I had an accident in the cab on the way to Arby's. Took off my unders in the backseat. Threw 'em out the window. They flew back in.

The cab driver freaked out 'cause I got "doo-doo" all over his car. Guess who calls #2 "doo-doo"? Black cab drivers when they want you dead.

I got kicked out of the cab with my peener and veggies all exposed. Hope there's no security video. They know me at Arb's. When you fill your pants in a cab on the way to a closed Arby's at 3 a.m., it's time to cut back to only light beer for a while, you guys. I need to go for a walk and think about my actions.

SUNDAY, NOVEMBER 20, 2011
I need some time for reflection.

MONDAY, NOVEMBER 21, 2011
Really lookin' forward to the Turkey Day weekend, you guys.

No need to put in any effort at work this week. It's a short week. Best to take it easy and gear up for the celebraish.

I've been workin' on plans for the Turkey Day feast. Might see what Ann and the kids are up to. Could help her stuff her bird. Ha! (Just some guy humor.)

Ann says I can stop by, but she cooks a terrible bird. Gonna really wow her when I bring over my brined bad boy. Just give hers to the neighbor's dog.

TUESDAY, NOVEMBER 22, 2011
Nosey Lady went bananas today and screamed, "Just 'cause it's a holiday week doesn't mean everyone can sit around pickin' their butt!" So inappropriate. If there's anyone who needs to pick their butt, it's Nosey Lady. Always looks like she's got half of Lane Bryant crammed in her backdoor.

Butt-picking is somethin' that should be done in private. Like the john, your car, or behind a shrub. That's always been my policy, you guys.

Left work early today to ice my bird and saw Dave had put cans of cold ones in the cooler with my brined raw turk. Idiot. Really steamed.

WEDNESDAY, NOVEMBER 23, 2011

Today Ken said to stop buggin' him so he could get some work done. I was tellin' him the true history of Turkey Day! Some people don't like learning. What kinda dumb corncob is doing actual work today? The Turkey Day celebraish is all about relaxation. You gotta ease into it.

Dave kept droppin' hints about "havin' nowhere to go tomorrow" and "hope BK is open." Told that sad bag o' crap he can come to Ann's.

If a pal's alone on a holiday, ya gotta take him in even if he's stupid garbage. Feels good to help out a slob with your charity, you guys.

3:32 A.M.

Woke up to take a whizz. Dave cut off one of the turk legs and microwaved it! Said he was takin' part of his "share" early. SUPER P.O.'d.

Had to cut the other leg off the turk to make it even. Gonna replace 'em with kielbasas. Actually think it'll be badass. Custom bold flavors.

THURSDAY, NOVEMBER 24, 2011

Turkey Day 2011. Never forget. Let's roll, you guys.

Sad to see the poor people lined up and fightin' for savings this morning. People should just work hard every day so you don't have to get up at 4 a.m. for a $30 TV.

Had a blast at Ann's. Flipped my bird on its end to create "The Mega Turk Bowl." Filled it with bacon, taters, corn, cheese, and stuffin'. It was so out of bounds. My son said, "Daddy's turkey's weird." No, weird is eatin' veggie chicken nuggets with ketchup and wearin' a stupid magic hat on Turkey Day.

It was actually great to have my man Dave at Ann's. Think more marriages would work out if you had a buddy to hang out with livin' with you. Dave pulled such a classic. He put the turkey neck in his fly and snuck up on Ann. She turned around and went bananas. Said it was inappropriate. When your wife doesn't crack up at a grown man with a turkey neck hangin' out of his pants like a peener, bein' separated makes a lot of sense.

No one would touch the Mega Turk Bowl, so me and Dave went at it alone. Was nice not to have to eat Ann's dried-out bland bird. For the holidays, if someone makes something you don't like, it's polite manners to let 'em know passively so they don't embarrass themselves again.

Me and Dave musta drank a thousand beers. Ann asked if we were ok to drive. She coulda just asked us to go. Such a rude hint. Plus, it's ok to drive drunk on Turkey Day. When everyone knows everyone else is bombed, the understanding is to just be extra careful, you guys.

Just called to ask Ann if I could stop by to pick up some lefties. There was a ton, but we were too bombed to pack 'em up and nothin' was cleaned or put away when we left. She said, "Yeah, and you left your marijuana cigarette in the guest bathroom," then hung up. I forgot me and Dave burned a J in the guest john. Wonder if Ann really wants me to come get it, plus some lefties?

SATURDAY, NOVEMBER 26, 2011

Stopped by Ann's for some lefties last night. She wouldn't answer the door. I called a bunch of times. No answer. I could even see her inside the window! I sat in the 'Bring and wailed on the horn in the driveway for like ten minutes. A bunch of neighbors came out, but no Ann. Pretty sick of her head games.

Might head back over to Ann's today. Give her a piece of my mind after a few cold ones or I might get too harsh. Cold ones lighten your attitude. Just because you're separated from your wife doesn't mean she can hog all the Turkey Day lefties.

SUNDAY, NOVEMBER 27, 2011

Went to Ann's last night to get my damn lefties. She wasn't home. Got really steamed. Kicked in the back door. Gonna have to lay low for a while.

There weren't even any lefties in the fridge. Either they hogged 'em all down or she threw 'em out 'cause they were "old." She always does that. So wasteful. I wouldn't even HAVE to kick down the door of a house I OWN if Ann didn't change the locks. Sick of this.

Gotta admit, it felt good to kick that door down. Like Seagal or Dalton from *Road House*.

MONDAY, NOVEMBER 28, 2011

Ann's been callin' all day. Said the house got broken into but nothing was stolen. Oh, NOW she knows how to work the phone. Lettin' it go to voicemail. Not my prob.

First off, I know Ann's not in danger 'cause I kicked the door down. Secondly, if nothing was stolen, why even bother me with it?

Ann just left another message. Something about "not caring about your family's safety." Whatever. Don't need this while I'm at work. What am I supposed to do about somethin' that happened yesterday?

Plus, if you own property, it's your right as an American to destroy it in any way you please, you guys.

TUESDAY, NOVEMBER 29, 2011

This mornin' I walked in on Nosey Lady tellin' one of the head honchos that I'm "not really pulling my weight." Dirty backstabber. Really steamed. Nosey Lady better watch HER back. Ol' Karl knows a thing or two about really burnin' someone down. I've got all kinds of dirt on that sow.

If someone is out to get you, it's important to be prepared for war. Gotta have enough ammo to really destroy their credibility, you guys.

WEDNESDAY, NOVEMBER 30, 2011

Happy Wing Wednesday, you guys. Brought my own hamburg bun, did some debonin', and made a McWing, B-Dubs style. Waitress gave me a look. Sometimes a bold flavor connoisseur can't be constrained by the limits of a restaurant's menu. You gotta make your own rules, you guys.

If McDonald's won't take advantage of my McWing idea, I'll just keep makin' 'em myself at B-Dubs. Every time I do, they lose a sale. Profits down the drain.

You could make a McWing with boneless wings, but it's not the same. Gotta debone 'em yourself. It's a labor of love and bold passion.

Plus, boneless wings are for sissies, women, and children. A real bold flavor man never orders boneless wings. Ever. That's a fact.

Finishin' up my dirt list on Nosey Lady. Gotta burn her down before Friday. That's when people get canned. Gotta really ruin her life.

THURSDAY, DECEMBER 1, 2011

Really lookin' forward to the weekend, you guys.

Got my list of Nosey Lady burn-downs all set to go in case she wants to go toe-to-toe. No one messes with Captain Karl. NO ONE!

1. Nosey Lady locked the bathroom and I had to take a massive BM behind the work Dumpster, then clean my backdoor with napkins from BK.

2. Nosey Lady wears ill-fitting clothing that is a distraction, and not in the good way like causing carnal desires which are healthy. Women with loose sloppers should make an effort to cover themselves. I can't focus on my work while feeling physically ill.

3. Nosey Lady's Michelina's Lean Gourmet meals give the workplace a horrid odor and show no class. We're trying to be civil here.

4. Nosey Lady gave Vernon the worst work space. Right by the john. Only a racist would seat a cool soul brother by the toilet, you guys.

5. I think Nosey Lady buys her slacks with a pre-wedge that's unpickable. There's no other excuse. Again, very distracting. Puke city.

6. Nosey Lady kept dangerous Activias in the fridge, which almost sent me to an early grave. It's a hazardous substance

and should not be tolerated. No one keeps guns at work. They can kill you. So can twelve Activias.

7. Nosey Lady seems pretty hard up for affection from a gentleman. Could make her snap at any time. She could kill us all. It's a fact. Ann made me watch some Lifetime crap once about this gal who was puke city in the bod and face department. Then someone got steamy and nude with her for some guy humor with his pals after too many cold ones and he videotaped it. When she found out, she murdered a bunch of innocent people. Pretty sure it'll happen to Nosey Lady sometime. Then we'll all be sorry. Let's make an effort to keep it safe.

In conclusion, do we really want a racist/possible murderer who's a grossout in our workplace? Let's at least get her the help she needs.

FRIDAY, DECEMBER 2, 2011

Just walked by Nosey. Gave her the "cut your throat" sign. She went and made a phone call. Think Nosey got my drift and took back what she said. The "cut your throat" sign is universal. Lets anyone know you mean business. Intimidation is the first rule of battle, you guys.

Just got a phone call from one of the head honchos. Supposed to have a lunch meetin' with him and Nosey on Monday. Somethin' big is up.

SATURDAY, DECEMBER 3, 2011

Dave just came out of his room in some weird fleece suit. Said it's called a "Forever Lazy." Think I'm gonna go for a walk now.

Big showdown with Nosey tomorrow. Before you go to war, you live life to the fullest. Really turn up the volume.

I'm drinkin' a Dewar's-and-Diet out of a goddamn Burger King cup. That's how a MOTOR CITY BAD BOY starts his Sunday. Feel like I could drink a thousand beers right now, you guys. Might get rocked like never before. To the Scorpions' "Hurricane" standards. Crankin' up some Seger. Feelin' SO good. If a pile of cold ones and "Roll Me Away" cranked up on a Sunday afternoon don't make you feel like a god, you don't deserve the USA.

Dave just said he's been thinkin' about killin' himself and is gonna lay off the booze. That's what happens when you wanna stop drinkin' and start wearin' a Forever Lazy. If I was Dave, I'd wanna kill myself too. No rockin' pony, no 'rang, no 'logne, no babes. What's the point? Just eat a barrel.

Wonder how many babes Ted Nugent made it with today? Probably at least three. Maybe four. Gonna tell Dave. Make him really hate himself.

When a pal is feelin' down, you have to show how much worse the future will be. Makes the present not seem so bad, you guys.

If I was gonna kill myself, I'd fly a helicopter into the sun. It'd be badass. Babes would weep for the carnal possibilities they'd missed.

Now Dave's in his room listening to *Dark Side of the Moon*. If you're gonna kill yourself, at least do it to Seger's *Beautiful Loser*. Have some taste.

Man, I'm so bombed. Flyin' SO high. I'VE GOT THE WORLD BY THE BALLS. EVERYONE CAN KISS MY SMELLY ASS. GO LIONS! I'M GONNA BURY THAT IDIOT TOMORROW!!! YOU

DON'T MESS AROUND WITH CAPTAIN KARL. I'M THE MAN!!! SUCK MY PEENER!!! If you're not with me, I could give a fat USA crap about what you think. And that's the bottom line 'CAUSE STONE COLD KARL WELZEIN SAYS SO. Kiss my ass. If you don't like me, I don't need you. You weak pile of garbage. Go back to your stupid life where people pretend to like you. 'M the friggin' man. YOU SUCK. That's my new motto. Let's roll. I'VE GOT TO STYLE AND PROFILE LIKE NEVER BEFORE! WOOOOO!!!! Goin' on the roof. Smoke some cigs. I'm the man.

If you choose to turn to the dark side, do so quietly and without reservation, you guys.

MONDAY, DECEMBER 5, 2011

Styled and profiled a little too hard last night. Tore the right mirror off the 'Bring. Put a big gouge down the side. It's really a mystery. Think it happened when I was tryin' to leave the Déjà Vu gentlemen's club last night. Probably happens to Ric Flair all the time.

Had my big lunch at Applebee's with Nosey and the honcho today. Went all out on my order. It's a power move, you guys. Started with the Wonton Chicken Tacos. Such a bold fusion masterpiece of Old Mexico and Oriental flavors. Then I moved on to the Shrimp 'n Parm Sirloin. Ordering the second most expensive item on the menu shows class, without being obnoxious.

All the blood went to my stomach from the eats so I went in the john to regroup, exhausted from stylin' and profilin'. Passed out on the can. Head Honcho came to see if I was ok but I played it off with some grunts.

When I came back to the table, Honcho said he wanted to have a talk with me and Nosey because she was "worried" about me. Something about "erratic" behavior. I told Nosey she was wrong about me bein' erratic. I'm erotic. Like when I was at Déjà Vu last night. Could tell Honcho agreed, guy-to-guy, but had to play it cool.

When Nosey went to the john, I knew I had my chance to bond with the big man. Told Honcho all about the rockin' chest beefers at the club last night. Guys love hearin' about beefers. Then I asked the Honcho if he was a bold flavor man? I made power move #2 and ordered us a couple ice-cold Sam Adams. Guy-to-guy. None for Nosey.

When Nosey Lady came back, I asked her if she fell in? Honcho put his head in his hands. He musta been DYIN' to crack up. She turned red and just blurted out asking if I have a drinkin' problem. So inappropriate. Got really steamed, pounded my cold one, and got another to show her I had control.

I told Nosey Lady SHE has the drinking problem and whoever smelt it dealt it. Gave Honcho a guy-to-guy "wink." Really shut her down.

Honcho wants to have another meeting in private after the holidays. Just a guy-to-guy. It's what alpha dogs do. Probably get to the nitty-gritty without Nosey buttin' in. Or maybe just have a cool hang?

When the check came, it was split three ways. Thought work would pick it up. Got really steamed. I wouldn't have gone all out with my order if I was payin'. Honcho could tell I was P.O.'d and paid for mine too. Nosey still had to pay for her own. Ha! She must have been so embarrassed at my success.

If someone wants to get you in trouble, you strike first and strike hard. Really bury 'em. It doesn't matter if you're at an Applebee's.

THURSDAY, DECEMBER 8, 2011

Really lookin' forward to the weekend, you guys.

We picked Secret Santas at work today. Wanted to get a good one. Nothin' worse than gettin' a grossout. Secret Santa is the time to reward someone and take credit on the sly or punish them anonymously so they know they suck super hard. Last year my Secret Santa got me a badass Red Wings scarf. It let me know I was on team "cool." Wish I didn't drop it in the toilet at Wendy's.

I drew Nosey Lady. Can hardly admit it to myself. Dave said, "Christmas is the time to treat your enemies with love just like Jesus did." Jesus helps BELIEVERS, not enemies, idiot. They can burn.

FRIDAY, DECEMBER 9, 2011

Rockin' around . . . the Friday tree . . . time to not, do, any work . . . Happy Friday to ya, you guys!

Feel like no one should have to work on Fridays around the holidays. Everyone's too busy gettin' pumped for the big celebraish.

Might round up Ken and Vernon and head to Chili's for a "gents only" lunch. Could be our own little Christmas tradish! We Three Kings are off to Chili's! Ha! Just made that up. Bold holiday flavors and top-shelf margs for the celebraish. The works. Super pumped! Pretty sure if Jesus was born in modern times, the Three Wise Men woulda brought the Christ Child some Chili's To Go, you guys.

SATURDAY, DECEMBER 10, 2011

Just woke up at home. Found a $179 receipt from Chili's in my billfold. Don't remember anything after going to Chili's. Kinda concerned, you guys.

Just called Ken and Vernon. No answers. Bet they're still hurtin' too. We musta really rocked it at Chili's. What a great start to the tradish.

I bet every year, when the "Gents Only Holiday Chili's Crew" walks into Chili's, they'll say, uh oh, here comes the fellas from Bad Boy City, USA.

Chili's should have a wall of fame. A pic of me, Ken, and Vernon all pointin' at the $179 tab would let everyone know we are NOT to be messed with.

SUNDAY, DECEMBER 11, 2011

Decided to get loose at Wild Spurs last night with Dave. My treat. Around the holidays, I like to really spread it around. Had such a blast. Got turned on to a new jam, Luke Bryan's "Country Girl (Shake It for Me)." It's pretty much a rockin' party jam that turns the party out and makes the gals go wild. Don't care who you are, "Country Girl" is a feel-good jam.

When "Country Girl" came on, Dave started doin' this dance he calls "The Peener." Pure pelvic thrusts. Really wild and carnal, you guys. Man, when Dave does "The Peener," it's time to clear off the dance floor, 'cause when he's on, he's pretty much the dirtiest player in the game. Dave was on fire. Then he just went for it with a deep tongue kiss to some overweight babe! Told him it's cool, mouths are all the same. Real proud of him.

As time goes by, for the most part, you only regret the things you DIDN'T do. Life is nothin' without stories to tell the next day, you guys.

MONDAY, DECEMBER 12, 2011

Ken and Vernon are actin' weird today. Wonder what went down at Chili's on Friday? Maybe they did somethin' after I blacked out?

Gonna go hang out by Vernon. See if I can get the scoop. When you need the 411, it's best to ask a soul brother with his ear to the streets.

11:25 A.M.

Vernon said I was really wildin' out at Chili's and he "don't even know" about me anymore. Guess I ordered a bunch of shots. Sounds about right. Guess Vernon and Ken didn't want any shots, so I said, "More for me." Vernon said I did like six before the food came, then took down a few margs. Then Ken ordered the Quesadilla Explosion Salad. Vernon said I started "makin' some nasty-ass bathroom jokes" about it. Well, you kinda HAVE to. I mean, the Chili's Quesadilla Explosion Salad makes you have to make a Quesadilla Explosion "Salad" afterward. Told Vernon it was just *real* talk.

Guess Ken got steamed and left. Vernon said I followed Ken out to his car makin' BM sounds at him. He almost ran me over 'cause I wouldn't move. Vernon told me I said I was glad Ken left so we could have a guy-to-guy. He said, "You got it all wrong, I ain't on the DL. Don't try none of that nasty crap you did to my boy Darryl at the club."

Guess I got P.O.'d at Vernon for not getting ribs. He said I kept going on about "bold soul tastes" and knocked a marg on the floor. Then I ordered two more racks of ribs and had three shots. He went back to work when I tried to show him "The Peener."

V-Dog said I never made it back there. When Nosey Lady asked where I was, he told her he didn't know. She said, "It doesn't matter. I don't care anyway."

Kinda remember still being at Chili's by myself. Think I went up to some tables and tried to show them "The Peener" too. Everyone better hold on to their hats, 'cause in no time, "The Peener" is gonna be the new dance craze that's sweepin' the nation, you guys. Dave invented "The Peener" a few years back, actually. But now it seems the time is right. Society is more open-minded to carnal dance crazes.

Relieved that Vernon gave me the 411. Sounds like we had a blast! I really rocked it, bad boy style. I don't always black out at Chili's, but why even go at all if you're not going to at least try? Especially during the bold holiday season.

TUESDAY, DECEMBER 13, 2011

Kid Rock was on Guy Fieri's *Diners, Drive-Ins and Dives!* It was so money! Watched it five times. Wonder what the ratings were? Probably bigger than "Who Shot J.R.?"

Looks like Kid Rock is really kickin' up some bold flavors in Clarkston, Michigan. Gonna have to make a trip. Maybe hang with the American Bad Ass. Kid Rock hangin' with Guy Fieri on Triple D is such a television milestone. Like when Stevie Wonder was jammin' with the Cosbys.

I really think me and Kid Rock could really hit it off. Right off the bat, we could compare rockin' pony adventures. Then, who knows? Kid Rock is into cold ones, chest beefers, bold flavors, and turnin' the party out. We're like brothers from another mother, you guys.

Maybe I should invite Guy and the Triple D crew to see how we do things around MY parts. Have him bring Kid. It'd be such a blast. There's other Chili's in the world, but I think the Flint location really has somethin' special. Feels like a real neighborhood joint.

WEDNESDAY, DECEMBER 14, 2011

Might have to start droppin' some hints for the big Secret Santa celebraish. Don't want to get some crap like the 3D puzzle I gave last year. If you don't ask for what you really want at Christmas, what you're really askin' for is somethin' to fill up your trash can, you guys.

Gonna send my wish list around at work. Nothin' wrong with a few "hints." Make it sound like we should all "share 'em for holiday fun."

Ol' Karl's been a good boy this year! Think my wish list rocks, you guys.

SATURDAY, DECEMBER 17, 2011

Looks like I ripped the door off the microwave last night. Found it on the floor with a note to myself.

Think I had an idea where microwaves didn't have doors and AC/DC was on the infomercial. Not THAT stupid, I guess. Could be a hit.

Don't feel well. Gonna go snooze in my car where it's cool and so, so quiet. Watch the snow come down. To sleep, perchance to dream, you guys.

12:35 A.M.

Woke up to Bruce's "The Rising." Really made some things make sense. Whether it's AIDS, a major terrorist attack, or why you ripped off the microwave door in a drunk blackout, Bruce Springsteen has the answer.

Why don't we just make Bob Seger and Bruce Springsteen the prez and VP? Only question is, who would be what? The USA could be so beautiful if that happened. "Born to run, against the wind—Springsteen/Seger 2012. Let's put America back in the White House, you guys." Who knows America more than Bruce Springsteen and Bob Seger?! It sure as shit ain't no corncob like Newt Romney. Ann always said Oprah should be president. So stupid. The economy would be all screwed with her giving away free cars and pajamas and crap.

SUNDAY, DECEMBER 18, 2011

Guess I called Jody last night. She just rang back. Said not to do that anymore. Called me a "psychopath." Ha! She wants me back. So bad.

Playin' hard-to-get with insults to a babe is a two-way street. Gonna call Jody now. Tell her she's the Butt Police of Asstown. So carnal.

5:35 P.M.

Jody didn't pick up. Left her a message: "You're the Butt Police of Asstown. Let's get erotic soon. You want my beef." Think I nailed it.

Gonna go on the roof and scream at the sky with Dave. Let everyone know we're #1. And bombed. Crankin' up the celebraish!

Goin' to lay down in the john. Feel just awful. Death would be a welcome warm blanket right now, you guys. I drink so much on Sundays 'cause I have to go to work on Monday. I'M not the problem. Work is. So if I need to sleep by the toilet for two hours, I'll do it.

TUESDAY, DECEMBER 20, 2011

Guess we're supposed to have the big Secret Santa celebraish tomorrow. Still don't know what to get Nosey Lady. Maybe 7-Eleven nachos? Nah, too nice.

This might be more up her alley:

Gonna really let that stinkbag know how I operate.

And it's only 10 bucks. When it's supposed to be a $20 gift and you get it on sale for 10 but it WAS $20 before, it really puts the "secret" into "Secret Santa." Can't decide what's a more insulting size to get Nosey Lady's shirt in, S or XL? Both are a solid burn, you guys.

WEDNESDAY, DECEMBER 21, 2011

Really gearin' up for the big Secret Santa celebraish. Only took down six Mango Habs for Wing Wednesday. Gotta take advantage of the free eats.

Wrapped Nosey Lady's gift in toilet paper. Ha! Not USED TP of course. It's important to show some class when insulting someone, you guys.

2:45 P.M.

Just took a sneak peek in the kitchen. There's TONS of goodies. No shrimp this year though. What's a holiday party without shrimp? Pretty steamed.

I'm gonna run to Kroger and get my own personal shrimp platter. It's gonna rock. Show everyone how I roll. Too bad, so sad, for everyone else.

3:20 P.M.

Got a bottle of Crown to go with my shrimp platter. Work only sprang for beer and wine. Hard booze for the holidays is the only way to celebrate. That's always been my policy. So pumped for the celebraish to start! When I walk into the party with my Crown and shrimp platter like a Christmas King, everyone'll go nuts. Probably get some high fives.

Writin' my name on the platter: "KARL'S SHRIMP." Don't need any freeloaders thinkin' it's part of the spread. People are so cheap.

Goin' in the john with my Crown for some pregame sippers. Gotta grunt out a BM preemie. Doo-doo free + a buzz = how to show up for a celebraish.

4:05 P.M.
Secret Santa Celebraish 2011. Let's roll, you guys. Time to show work how the Christmas King from Bad Boy City, USA, rocks the party!

THURSDAY, DECEMBER 22, 2011

Got a pretty mean buzz on before the celebraish yesterday. The preemie took longer to grunt out than expected so I had to hit the Crown hard. Figured it'd relax me. Then I went to get my shrimp platter so I could make a rock star entrance with shrimp AND my Crown. Some selfish idiot already put the shrimp out for EVERY-ONE. So steamed.

MY shrimp platter said "KARL'S SHRIMP" on it. It wasn't for EVERYONE. Maybe invite only VIP homeys like Vernon, but that's it. Half were already gone. I started askin' everyone if they ate some of my shrimp and if they did to cough up some cash. No one fessed up. WELL, IT DIDN'T JUST DISAPPEAR!

Started hoardin' a bunch of goodies and sneakin' 'em out to my car. No cash for my shrimp? I have to make things even. Fair's fair.

The only thing more insulting than stealin' another man's shrimp around the holidays is havin' carnal passions with his wife under his Christmas tree, you guys.

Was puttin' a cheese ball in my car when Nosey Lady opened her shirt. Guess she LOVED it and told everyone it was the right size. It was a SMALL! Liar.

I don't even wanna talk about what my Secret Santa gift was. Some a-hole got me a XXXL tee and some BK napkins. I KNOW what that means. XXXL means "Hey, tubs, Merry Christmas, slob!" and BK napkins mean "Go take another crap behind the Dumpster!" Leave it in the past. It was an accident. So cruel. I had to save face, so I challenged everyone to a "Chug the Crown & Do 'The Peener' " contest. A test of bold booze enjoyment and carnal body moves. No one wanted to join in. Losers. They'll be sorry next year when it's sweepin' the nation.

When I was chuggin' the Crown and doin' "The Peener," some people got out their phones for pics. Kinda felt like a rock star so I went extra hard. Kinda pulled my back and crashed into the snack buffet. Burned my stomach on a Crock-Pot. Guess it was kinda badass?

Got Lit'l Smokies BBQ sauce all over my shirt. But that's just the price of the bold bad boy lifestyle. Had to change into the XXXL tee. It had zero sex appeal, so I tore the sleeves off to let everyone see that my bod didn't need a XXXL. And I wanted to be lookin' good for Chili's.

Guess I dropped my wallet in the Crock-Pot crash so I sat in the 'Bring at Chili's and just finished my Crown. Almost as good as bein' inside? Whether you're poundin' whiskey in the parking lot by yourself or actually sittin' in the bar, Chili's just always feels right, you guys.

FRIDAY, DECEMBER 23, 2011

Really lookin' forward to the holiday weekend, you guys. Wonder what's on tap for the big celebraish? Might have to head out to do some shoppin' soon. Heard there's still plenty of time to get great gifts at Kohl's.

I gotta see what's up with Ann and the kids. Should probably see the fam at Christmas. It's not ideal, but it gives 'em a thrill when Santa Karl goes big. When it comes to gifts, I have it down. Always get people what YOU think they should get, not what THEY want. It makes 'em a better person, which is like a BONUS gift.

Think I'm gonna have a few cold ones before headin' to Kohl's. It helps you deal with all those rude sows fightin' for deals. Gotta burn 'em down right away.

Kohl's should sell shoppin' brewskis called "Kohl Ones." Maybe put in a bar for guys called "Kohl One City." It could save relationships.

7:42 P.M.

Talked to the manager at Kohl's about "Kohl One City." He didn't get it. Idiot. Had to get in his face. He asked if I was drunk. So rude.

The Kohl's manager said he was too busy to hear my idea. I said, "What? Managing KOHL'S? It's a cake job for dropouts!" What a no-vision loser.

He tried to walk away, so I did the arm block against the wall and said, "Listen, buddy . . ." (People know you mean biz when you say that.)

So anyway, I said, "Listen, buddy, 'Kohl One City' is a million-dollar idea. Don't force me to go to corporate. You'll be managin' a Payless, corncob."

Security escorted me out of Kohl's. I wasn't KICKED out. It's different. I was in the right. The security guard looked embarrassed for having to do it.

Gonna have to go back tomorrow. Hope that Kohl's manager joker isn't there.

SATURDAY, DECEMBER 24, 2011

5:37 P.M.

Just got back from Kohl's. Real disaster. Forgot my wallet fell out of my pants in the Crock-Pot crash. Only have $3 left in my pocket.

Had a nice gift spread picked out too. I told the cashier I'd come back with a check. I'm obviously good for it. She went and got that corncob manager. Told me I need an ID to use a check. Got so steamed.

The Kohl's manager offered to call a shelter for me in the spirit of Christmas. Then called me "brother." I'm not a homeless black man, idiot!

Just asked Dave if I could borrow some cash. Said he only has a 20 to last him for the weekend. He's such a lowlife. I should just take it from him. What's he gonna do to stop me? Nothin', that's what.

8:37 P.M.

Kinda bummed. Down to two cold ones. Gonna max out my $3 and change on Steel Reserve, then figure it out, *Man vs. Wild* style.

At least I'm feelin' good about the Lions havin' a big win today. It's makin' this Steel Reserve go down SO smooth. Well, smoother. It's not really that smooth. But definitely smoother.

Dave just put a DiGiorno in the oven. Oh. Yeeaah. Time to get the celebraish rockin'! Sure am hungry. Might have to sneak a couple slices.

I'm down to a Little Debbie Oatmeal Creme, a frozen Tina's bean burreet, half a Steel, and half a can of Chunky Soup that's been open in the fridge for I don't know how long.

9:15 P.M.

Great, Dave's hoggin' the DiGiorno. Folded the whole thing in half. He says it's how they do it in NYC and won't share. So steamed. Like Dave's ever been to NYC.

10:34 P.M.

Ann's not returning my calls. Probably busy gettin' ready for the big celebraish. We'll just hook up tomorrow, I guess.

12:05 A.M.

Fishin' Dave's DiGiorno crusts out of the trash. It's a sin to be wasteful on Christmas Eve with all the starving people, otherwise this wouldn't be my style. WWJD, you know? I'd personally never eat out of the trash. I have class. But it's a holiday. Helping the poor is basically a gift to the baby Jeez.

1:32 A.M.

Hittin' the sack. Gonna figure it out tomorrow. There's still plenty of time for great gifts? May visions of bold flavors dance in your heads.

SUNDAY, DECEMBER 25, 2011–CHRISTMAS DAY

Merry Christmas, you guys.

Might head down to the soup kitchen. See if they need a hand and maybe get a bite for myself. Really take 'em to Flavor Town.

MONDAY, DECEMBER 26, 2011

Had a blast at the soup kitchen yesterday, you guys. They already had enough hands on deck, so I just got to hang out. What a celebraish!

I brought a bunch of my own hot sauces, condiments, and special seasonings. It made that soup kitchen grub off the chain! Told the soup kitchen director, let's guy-to-guy about the next celebraish. Make it Bold City. He told me I should get an evaluation, so I think it's on. He gave me an OFFICIAL government address to go "talk to someone." Sounds hush-hush. Philanthropy is serious biz.

I was rappin' with a soul brother from the streets named Peanut when I remembered I still had my trunk liquor. It was basically a Christmas miracle. He said he wasn't "s'posed to be drinkin'," but I insisted. Even if you're "not s'posed to be drinkin'," it don't count on holidays. Ann never called back yesterday. Whatever. Dave even ditched me to go somewhere with his 20 bucks. Whatever. Me and Peanut were just fine keepin' it rockin' with trunk liquor at the pad.

Peanut kept talkin' about "not wantin' to live no more." Looks like I was his Christmas angel, so I just kept feedin' him shots. They're good for the soul. Peanut said he "been around the way for a minute and ain't got no good on the horizon." Man, he talks SO cool. Kinda like John Fogerty.

When Peanut passed out and wet himself, he looked peaceful like a baby. Felt like I truly did somethin' GOOD this Christmas. Hallelujah to the USA, you guys.

ACKNOWLEDGMENTS

Thanks:

Van Halen with the Red Rocker AND Diamond Dave. Any REAL man
  keeps it rockin' with both.

Stone Cold Steve Austin, can I get an aw hell yeah!

The USA.

My main man Guy Fieri, and the Triple D crew.

Cold ones.

The Detroit Tigers.

Sparky Anderson, RIP.

The Detroit Pistons, "the Bad Boys."

The Detroit Lions. Get your crap together. Sick of this.

Taco Bell.

Dave, I guess. Not sure.

My bro Al.

Little Caesar's.

Mr. McMahon, "YERRRR FIRED!" (Ha!)

Over the Top. Such a great flick.

7-Eleven.

Ric Flair, "WOOOOOO!"

Macho Man Randy Savage, RIP, brother.

The Dayton Family, MC Breed (RIP), Esham, and Mack the Jacka.

Filet-O-Fish Fridays.

Bold Flavors.

Ken? Not sure.

Tony Bourdain. What happened to your 'rang? So badass.

Kayfabe.

The American Dream, Dusty Rhodes, daddy.

The McRib.

Top-shelf margs. So smooth.

Vernon.

Crazy Cooter (don't want him to murder me for not puttin' his name in here).

Chili's.

'Bee's.

That CM Punk guy. Pretty cool.

Penthouse mag.

Triple H. Why'd you cut off your rockin' pony? Kinda concerning.

Kirk "Gibby" Gibson (fist pumps).

Bruce Springsteen, The Boss.

Dalton from *Road House.*

Grand Blanc, MI. Flint, MI, Saginaw, MI. Bay City, MI. Everyone in MI, really.

Pat Brice. The Laddy. "Like a pitbull barking in your goddamn ear."

Lance Parrish.

The 'Bring.

Kathy Ireland. So smokin'.

Maui Jim shades.

Kohl's, for great style AND value.

Ted Nugent, "the Motor City Madman."

Jim Beam.

Kid Rock.

Crown & Diet.

3:57 in "Still of the Night" by Whitesnake.

Paddy McGee's Irish Pub.

Koegel's hot dogs.

Spatz bread.

Vernors ginger ale.

Peanut.

Chest beefers on the thick and all-natural babes from coast to coast, piled high with all the toppings.

Special Mention?
My fam. Gotta do the right thing. I can't help it if they didn't want pretty much the Dad of the Year in their life anymore. Guess I cared too much. Don't know if I should leave this in. Kinda bombed. Again, just tryin' to do the right thing.

Extra-Special Thanks:
Bob Seger & the Silver Bullet Band, and, you guys.

No Thanks:
Doug & Tina Carlson and Nosey Lady. Suck it, corncobs.